THE CHURCH MILITANT

THE CHURCH MILITANT

By *Harold A. Bosley*, Ph.D.

THE CARNAHAN LECTURES

HARPER & BROTHERS — PUBLISHERS
New York

THE CHURCH MILITANT

FIRST EDITION

A-B

Library of Congress catalog card number 51-11886

TO

B. Foster Stockwell

A "Fighting Angel"

Contents

Preface

The honor of giving the first series of lectures on the Carnahan Lectureship is as exacting as it is overwhelming. For, clearly, it is intended and destined to become one of the major lectureships sponsored by Christian seminaries and divinity schools anywhere in the world. I am confident that the years ahead will justify both the intention and the prophecy. It will remain one of the great satisfactions of my life to have been present at, and to have had a part in, the launching of so auspicious an undertaking.

There is a real sense of fitness in the fact that the Carnahan Lectureship is placed under the direction of the Facultad Evangélica de Teología in Buenos Aires. Carrie Jay Carnahan and Ella May Carnahan, the sisters in whose honored memory the lectureship was established, were devoted members of the Methodist Church in the United States and deeply and continuously interested in the work of the Evangelical churches in Latin America. They were particularly interested in the Facultad Evangélica de Teología as the center for training leaders in the work of the schools and churches. Through the years they gave generously of their prayers, time, efforts and money toward the expansion of the plant and program of the school. It is fitting that this Lectureship should bear their name.

The seminary is interdenominational, with eight different church groups represented in its student body. It is a good

omen for the future of the ecumenical movement in Latin
America that this is so. It is the best guarantee now in view
that the Christian work in South America will not get hopelessly lost in the maze of denominational and sectarian rivalry.

If, in some of the lectures, I seem to center attention upon
the Methodist Church, there are two reasons for it—and neither
grows out of a sectarian interest or intention. (1) The Methodist Church is the one I know best; I feel freer to make critical
judgments of it than of any other church, and I am more
certain that the praise which I direct toward it is deserved.
(2) The lectures are devoted to the almost impossible attempt
to catch and convey the sense of dynamic motion in the Church
Militant. This requires a centering of attention upon certain
periods and using them as a watchtower, so to speak, from
which we observe developments in the Christian tradition. I
have chosen three periods or phases in Christian history for this
purpose: New Testament life and times; the Reformation; and
the Methodist movement. If I were as familiar with the Presbyterian, Congregational-Christian, Disciples, or Baptist heritage
as I am with the Methodist, any one of them could have been
used for the third "Watchtower" with equal fitness. William
Warren Sweet's four-volume series on *Religion on the American
Frontier,* studying the Baptists, the Presbyterians, the Congre-
gationalists, and the Methodists, makes this abundantly plain.
And I am convinced by my trip around Latin America that
the material for a later volume is being written in the life and
deeds of the Christian leaders of those countries.

The first six chapters constitute the Carnahan Lectures. The
last four are a series of sermons presenting the meanings and
claims of the church. All ten were given in the course of one
year's preaching at the First Methodist Church of Evanston.
I am including in this book both the poems and various personal references to individual experiences and churches that
were in the sermons but not in the lectures as delivered in the

Seminary. Poetry is the bane of even an excellent interpreter, and the experiences localized in this country were not always useful illustrative material in South America. I cannot believe that the frequent direct references to the church in which, and the congregation to which, I was preaching the sermons will be misunderstood or misconstrued as evidence of a parochial concern by any preacher or layman. As a preacher it is my plain duty to be concrete, specific and personal in what I say from the pulpit. I have retained as much of this emphasis as seemed advisable.

Needless to say, I appreciate the fact that the First Methodist Church of Evanston, Illinois, granted me leave of absence from my duties in order to make the trip to South America. I accepted this without anxiety because the direction of the church was in the competent hands of my colleagues on the staff. This is but another way in which I am indebted to them.

HAROLD A. BOSLEY

First Methodist Church
Evanston, Illinois

THE CHURCH MILITANT

1 The Tradition of the Church:
Fighting Angels

SCRIPTURE LESSON

Now when they saw the boldness of Peter and John, and perceived that they were unlearned and ignorant men, they marvelled; and they took knowledge of them, that they had been with Jesus.

And beholding the man which was healed standing with them, they could say nothing against it.

But when they had commanded them to go aside out of the council, they conferred among themselves,

Saying, What shall we do to these men? for that indeed a notable miracle hath been done by them is manifest to all them that dwell in Jerusalem; and we cannot deny it.

But that it spread no further among the people, let us straitly threaten them, that they speak henceforth to no man in this name.

And they called them, and commanded them not to speak at all nor teach in the name of Jesus.

But Peter and John answered and said unto them, Whether it be right in the sight of God to hearken unto you more than unto God, judge ye.

For we cannot but speak the things which we have seen and heard.

So when they had further threatened them, they let them go, finding nothing how they might punish them, because of the people: for all men glorified God for that which was done.

THE ACTS 4:13-21

I

MOST of us would agree that it is a good thing ancestor worship died out of our religious tradition a long time ago; so long ago, in fact, that it is difficult to find more than a few fugitive traces of it in the Old Testament. This is all to the good—if we may believe the clear verdict of history. Religions which tolerate, much less depend upon, ancestor worship in any form are, of necessity, backward rather than forward looking. They permit yesterday not so much to influence as to determine tomorrow. They call to mind the fable of the bird who was so impressed with where he had been that he learned to fly backward, the better to enjoy his achievement longer.

But when we reject ancestor worship we do not thereby reject our ancestors, much less the wisdom won and imbedded in ancestral experience. Rather, we honor and respect them where honor and respect are due. But we do not revere them; we do not deify them; we do not put them on a pedestal and fall down before them; we do not accept their any and every word on any and every issue as the norm for our thinking and living. They do not deserve—and I know of no set of ancestors who do deserve—indiscriminate praise.

All of which is an introduction to the statement that this series of studies in the Church Militant is intended to be an essay in critical appreciation. They spring from a sense of profound gratitude to the men and the women who through the centuries have both treasured the insights of religion and been able to perpetuate them through the Church. We owe these people an incalculable debt—no one can fairly deny that. It is impossible to imagine what our life would be like today had they not done as they did. The least we can say is this: it would be unrecognizably different because it would have been molded by different moral standards and directed toward different moral goals.

Our spiritual ancestors, we shall find, were a sturdy lot. When I think of them I am reminded of Pearl Buck's description of her missionary father—Fighting Angel. They are the soul—the living, eternal soul—of the Church Militant. Yet, in real life, they were uncomfortably like us. Not so much as we are, perhaps, but as we ought to be, and under God, could be. They were ordinary people made extraordinary by their devotion to the will of God as they found it in Jesus Christ. Their lives and efforts were a crisscross of good and evil, strength and weakness, lucid insight and incredible blindness. That, better than anything else, explains why the tradition which they molded and perpetuated and which we have inherited must be treated with critical appreciation.

We come to this task, not in pride but in humility; not in the spirit of condescension but out of our deep need for help. For we know how sadly we need every ounce of goodness, strength and insight we can find in it as we seek to live in a world which seems bent on suicide. This, I am sure, is one of the most compelling reasons why all branches of the Christian Church are turning to the same task. It was a sound instinct that caused the World Council of Churches to center its attention, from the very outset of its historic career, upon the faith, the life and the work of the Church. The Methodist Church, in whose ministry I have the honor to serve, has called upon her people to pay special attention to these matters at the present time.

Since the phrase, the Church Militant, may be unfamiliar to some, a word of explanation may be in order at the very outset. Traditionally, the history of the life and work of the Church has been regarded as falling into two stages: the Church Militant and the Church Triumphant.

The Church Militant is the Church at work in the redemption of the world. The Church Triumphant is the Church whose work is done. The Church Militant knows that she lives in a world that is dying of sin, of alienation from God, and believes it to be her divine commission to confront that world with the gospel claim that in Jesus Christ we have "the way, the truth, and the life" which alone, when accepted and followed, can lead us to a new day. The Church Triumphant, by contrast, will be the ideal state of the Church when she has accomplished her mission, when, like the Good Shepherd, she has brought her entire family to the safety of One Fold.

The permanent tragedy of the Christian Church is the ease with which she has confused the Church Militant with the Church Triumphant, is the way in which and the readiness with which she has sought to be at rest in an unredeemed world. Impregnated by evil herself in so many ways, she has chosen to pretend virtue rather than repent of her sins. Surrounded by the entrenched evils of society in all ages, she has been noticeably tempted either to ignore them or to rationalize them rather than to issue a resounding call to repentance.

Here in this world as it is where we all have sinned and come short of the glory of God, where our sins always find us out, the Church is and must forever be the Church Militant, the Church at work in the redemption of the world; the Church that will not, because she cannot, rest until in the Providence of God, that end is won. When this is spelled out in concrete tasks in our world today, there is an enormous temptation to write it all off as a quixotic adventure, as a futile and foolish charge of a brigade of light-headed idealists. The only adequate antidote to that feeling of defeatism—and it is a sure cure— is to renew acquaintance with this tradition of "Fighting Angels" in which we are called to serve. See the Church Militant in courageous, aggressive, purposive action in eras that seemed as dark for those who lived in them as ours does to us today, and you will begin to hear the mighty roll of the drums of God above and beyond yet always within the tumult of these times.

II

Look for a moment at a panorama of the general history of the Christian Church, and you will find yourself studying an epic without parallel in the records of our civilization. The Church began as an obscure, persecuted sect in a small country at the eastern end of the Mediterranean and, through nineteen hundred years, grew into a world-girdling movement. It centers its life and faith in One who was killed as a trouble-maker yet who, today, confronts mankind as the only hope of a world being done to death by troubles of our own making.

As you would expect, the Church has been on the march almost steadily since her inception. Time after time she has struck her tents and moved out to new fields with her gospel. Starting out as an unwanted stepchild of Judaism, she early discovered that she had to make a choice between eking out a precarious existence as a Jewish sect or breaking her racial and cultural ties with Judaism and appealing to all men everywhere. The struggle between those who preferred to stay bound and those who wanted to go free, while brief, was intense enough to appear throughout the New Testament. Yet the issue seems never to have been in doubt. The divine commission to go to the ends of the earth was ringing in the ears of all who heard the call of Christ, and finally it drowned out the fears of the faint-hearted.

This is the Church Militant: not passively accepting and acquiescing in even a great religious tradition but seizing it aggressively and adapting it decisively until it serves present and future needs. At the very heart of the Church Militant were people like that remarkable couple, Priscilla and Aquilla— about whom we know very little, but that little is fascinating. So far as we know, their home was the center of a thriving Christian group in Ephesus and Rome. Traveling preachers like Paul, Peter and Apollos stopped with them. Not only did this

energetic, consecrated couple entertain the preachers, they
checked up on their theology. At least, they did that for Apollos
who seems to have been veering back toward the ties of tradi-
tionalism. Paul mentions them affectionately in his letters. We
get so in the habit of thinking that every important thing is
done on a gigantic scale and in the floodlight of world attention that it is good for us to see in Priscilla and Aquilla the
Church Militant.

We do well to think immediately of Paul when we think
about New Testament times. He is the incarnation of the
Church at work in the redemption of the world. Born in Asia
Minor of devout Jewish parents, he went to Jerusalem to become a Pharisee of the Pharisees. But he met Jesus Christ
instead, and heard his imperious call. In answer to it, Paul
went to his homeland, to Palestine, to every province of the
Roman Empire that bordered the northern shore of the Mediterranean, to Rome, and he was planning to go to Spain when
death sealed his ministry. He was always on the move; there
was always somewhere else to go, some other Macedonian call
to answer.

Though the spread of the New Faith was a miracle of speed,
it was bought at so great a price that we are hardly able to
comprehend it at this range. Paul's calm recital of his sufferings; the horrifying insights contained in the book of Revelation; the sickening descriptions of torture which come to us
from that period; the rioting and persecution at the hands of
established religious cults; the number and grimness of the
waves of persecution which the Roman Empire finally hurled
at the Christians—all this lies back of the two sentences with
which Will Durant concludes his tremendous book, *Caesar and
Christ:*

There is no greater drama in human record than the sight of a
few Christians, scorned and oppressed by a succession of emperors,
bearing all trials with a fierce tenacity, multiplying quietly, building

order while their enemies generated chaos, fighting the sword with the word, brutality with hope, and at last defeating the strongest state that history has known. Caesar and Christ had met in the arena, and Christ had won.

But the Church Militant was not through when she took the Roman Empire into receivership. Her missionaries fanned out to the north, east and west among the peoples who had come only partially, if at all, under the civilizing rule of Rome. They followed the Roman roads as far as the roads went, then they took to the rivers and forest trails. Wherever men were they went. And when the ships of Spain, Portugal, France and England struck westward in search of new worlds, these intrepid evangelists—Catholic and Protestant alike—were aboard. When, in due time, the ships came home with their fur traders and explorers, the evangelists were not there—they were teaching and preaching the gospel, sometimes writing a famous chapter of history, sometimes simply disappearing into the wilderness never to be heard from again. You need not approve of the fanaticism and bigotry which characterized many of them and which have left their exploits under so dark a shadow to thank God for them all, and for a faith that makes man march!

III

It is a good thing men like Luther, Zwingli, Calvin and Knox were "Fighting Angels." If they had been anything less, the Reformation would have died at birth. Their faith called for marching, though not over land and sea. They felt compelled of God to march against the enormous power of the Roman Catholic Church at those points where they believed it to be in error, and against the Holy Roman Empire which was supporting the Church, right or wrong. It took courage to lift up the Bible and say: "The Word of God is to be found in this book rather than in the words of the Pope." It took courage to

survey the sacramental system of the Church and say, "We will
keep only the sacraments that have a foundation in Scripture."
It took a tremendous faith in God and man to challenge the
power of the priesthood by proclaiming "the priesthood of all
believers." It took scholarly insight as well as courage to translate the Bible from Latin into the language of the people and
make it available for wide-scale reading and study. Tyndale
was burned for doing it—and Luther would have suffered the
same fate, if his enemies had had half a chance.

About 1730 the same compulsion to march fell upon a group
of sincerely religious students at Oxford University among
whom were John and Charles Wesley. They felt called of God
to challenge the evils of their day. First, they sought to purify
their own lives in order that they might become acceptable
messengers of God. Then, with relentless consistency, they
sought to purify all else. They reproached the Church for the
toleration of evils in her own life as well as in public life. They
tackled the sins of society. To a clergy, many of whom loved
and knew the joys of an easy life, they recommended fasting
and abstinence. To a Church that enjoyed the support and
esteem of the upper classes, they recommended a new and
profound concern for those in need: debtors, prisoners, widows
and orphans. Upon a ruling class that loved and exploited its
prerogatives to the full, they sternly urged the duty of providing a godly example for the people. Bible in hand, they and
their recruits went the length and breadth of their homeland
with a zeal that, to this day, seems unbelievable. Many of them
broke under the rigors of their efforts, but not before they had
set all England astir. Angry, frightened churchmen closed their
churches to these "fanatics," but the open fields lay close by,
and the meetings were held there. An early history of Methodism contains these vivid lines:

. . . in scores of places the Methodists were mobbed while holding services in the public streets and at their own houses. In some towns rioting lasted for a week, and the sufferings of the early martyrs were paralleled. Frequently parish ministers promoted the mobs, and magistrates were not willing to protect the Methodists. . . . Wesley . . . states of one such scene that he found a great mob, and after spending an hour taming them, exhorted them for two hours more.

I must say that I myself find no difficulty accepting at face value Wesley's conclusion that at the end of this three-hour treatment, "The ringleaders promised to make no further disturbance." [1]

Inevitably, these marching men found their way overseas and to America. The spirit in which they were sent and in which they came is best revealed in the brief note with which John Wesley sent George Shadford forth:

DEAR GEORGE:
The time has arrived for you to embark for America. . . . I let you loose, George, on the great continent of America. Publish your message in the open face of the sun, and do all the good you can.
Yours affectionately,
J. WESLEY.

There's a marching order for you. It gives a clear notion of what has been going on ever since. The chapter headings of William Warren Sweet's book *Methodism in American History* simply itemize one of the most stirring chapters in Church history: "Methodism Founded in America"; "Organizes for a Great Task"; "Invades New England"; "Crosses the Alleghenies"; "Keeps Pace with the Westward March"; "Shares in the Missionary Enterprise"; "Begins Her Educational Task"; "Faces the Civil War and Aftermath"; "Sounds the Social Gospel." And we are engaged in writing the next chapter today.

[1] Buckley, *American Church History,* V, 87.

It should bear the title: "Helps Mankind Face Its Most Fateful Hour." At the first Annual Conference of the Methodist church in 1773 we had 1,160 members in America, less than half the number of members in many of the great churches of our denomination today. This is the way they were distributed: 180 in New York; 180 in Philadelphia; 200 in New Jersey; 100 in Virginia; 500 in Maryland. One hundred and seventy-four years later this same church at its General Conference in Boston reported upwards of 9,000,000 people in its membership. Today the figure stands close to 10,000,000.

If anyone anywhere has reason to be humbly proud of his church, we have of ours. Here, in brief, are some of the reasons for our pride.

Ours is a Church which began as a movement within the Established Church of England but had the courage to resist the crippling influence of that Church and launch out on her own. One of my colleagues in the ministry of the Protestant Episcopal Church in Baltimore was reading a paper on the history of his church to a small group of ministers from various denominations. In the discussion that followed, he was asked, "What was the greatest mistake made in the history of your church?" Without a moment's hesitation he answered, "Forcing the Methodist movement to become a separate church." It goes without saying that few leaders in the Methodist movement wanted to start a separate church. Wesley was shocked at the idea and never let it happen while he was alive. He took a dim view of the determination of the Methodists in America to start a separate church and, although he did not oppose it, he never gave it his open blessing. But, given the situation which prevailed then, the break with the Established Church had to come—and it took a confident, consecrated leadership to do it.

Ours is a Church which has had few doctrinal troubles.

From Wesley's day on, freedom has prevailed in these matters. "Think and let think" has been the motto. We have not been careless in matters of belief, as the editors of *Life* magazine blandly said some time ago. While praising the Methodist Church for its dynamic life, they dubbed us "activists" and pointed out that we had paid all too little attention to our beliefs. It is a temptation to charge this criticism off to the Presbyterianism of Mr. Luce and say that only a Presbyterian completely anesthetized by the doctrine of predestination could have fathered the idea—but we must resist the temptation. Mr. Luce is quite right in saying that we do not come at people creed-end-to, so to speak. We have felt that matters of belief and differences on doctrine are tremendously difficult and important, and have tried to create a situation in which they can truly be approached, discussed and understood. We have had plenty of doctrinal debate, and the end is not yet, but we have had it on the firm foundation of a warm fellowship. We have learned through a few bitter experiences that heresy hunts are utterly vicious both in intention and consequence, and if I do not wholly misunderstand the temper of our Church, we are through with them. We shall continue our efforts to clarify our basic beliefs, to teach them to our members and our children, to present them to the world as our faith—of this you may be sure. But, in addition, we shall continue to stress the primacy and the necessity of fellowship one with another as the basis for all belief.

We shall not shrink from the title "activistic" which *Life* magazine and others may want to pin on us. We welcome it, we are prepared to insist upon it. We have tried to be "doers of the word." We have been preachers, teachers, travelers, makers, builders of churches, hospitals, schools, and mission stations all over the world.

Ours is a Church which, from the outset, has followed the

frontier. Wherever men were she has gone; she has used every
known device of presenting the gospel, and then added a few
of her own. She used a revivalism and every other technique
of mass emotional appeal as long as they seemed to be useful,
and discarded or modified them when they were not. I for
one do not feel called upon to apologize for the continuing
evangelistic appeal of our Church. Quite to the contrary, I am
compelled by conviction to emphasize it. It has been and continues to be the lifeblood of our mission. When we lose or
disown it we had better shut up shop and leave the field to
institutions better fitted than we are to sanctify the status quo
by confronting men with a message designed to ease their conscience rather than to save their souls. To borrow the words
with which Richard Baxter, a famous British preacher, described
the urgency of his message, our tradition requires us to preach
as "a dying man to dying men," to confront a civilization whose
sands have all but run out with the deep certainty that we
must be prepared to take Jesus Christ seriously as the way,
the truth, and the life—or perish at our own hand. *We preach
this message from conviction, and we preach it for decision.*

We are a frontier Church. The going has been hard and it
will always be hard whether we are taking the gospel to the
Indians in the Andes, or maintaining Newberry Center in
Chicago, or championing every effort to clean up the life, the
laws and the government of our own city and country, or trying to get a hearing for the voice of peace and brotherhood in
the councils of the nations. Let the frontier be geographical in
nature, or let it be in the social, economic and international
problems of our common life—we belong there or nowhere.

We have no reason to be discouraged with our traditional
policy of following the frontier. Bishop Ivan Lee Holt has re-
cently written a book that every discouraged Methodist ought

to read: *The Methodists of the World.* It opens with these lines:

The Methodist Church is the youngest of all the great Christian bodies, yet is the largest of all the Churches, that enjoy no favored connections with a political state. In the past two hundred years more people have voluntarily joined some Methodist Church after reaching years of discretion than any other religious body. It is represented in every continent and in nearly every nation. The Methodists are united in doctrine and they share a common history and tradition and they embrace nearly fifteen million adherents.[2]

I suggested earlier that we are now engaged in writing another chapter for Dr. Sweet's book on *Methodism in American History,* one entitled "Helps Mankind Face Its Most Fateful Hour." Methodists are not alone in this tremendous task, nor are we trying to do it alone. We are seeking and will continue to seek an ever-deepening and widening unity with other churches both in the National Council of Churches and in the World Council of Churches. The compulsion to march against the kind of denominationalism that weakens our every effort now rests heavily upon men in every segment of the circle of the Christian tradition.

And well it might! The things that unite Christian churches are much more important than those that separate them. The really serious challenges that face any one of them face all of them. The task of providing spiritual leadership for a world that is rapidly losing all sense of direction cannot be successfully attempted by any one of them—in fact, it is an open question as to whether it can be done by all of them working in the closest kind of unity. But if it can be done, you may be sure it will be because the great tradition of the Church Militant has come alive in all churches once more.

[2] P. 9.

IV

Against this background of the Church on the move—geographically, denominationally and interdenominationally—it is possible to single out three central characteristics of the Church Militant:

1. It is a Church with a purpose—a clear, compelling purpose: a divine purpose; one that comes to her trembling, fearful hands from the steady hand of God; a purpose that sets her apart from all other institutions known to men, yet one that plants her life and work squarely at the heart of human history.

2. It is a Church with a program—a comprehensive, vital, adaptable program that provides an intelligent and persuasive presentation of the purpose.

3. It is a Church with courage: the courage to believe in and be guided by her divine purpose; the courage to support and extend her program to every area of human need; the courage to rethink both purpose and program as need arises.

A Church like that will be ready and willing to be God's instrument in the redemption of the world. She will be able to work steadily and creatively at her task both on the world scene and in terms of local communities.

Eight years before his death, John Wesley wrote a brief essay on "Thoughts on Methodism." It opens with these solemn words:

I am not afraid that the people called Methodists should ever cease to exist in Europe or America; but I am afraid lest they should only exist as a dead sect, having the form of religion without the power, and this undoubtedly will be the case unless they hold fast to the doctrine, spirit and discipline with which they first set out.

What a tragedy it is when that dire prophecy comes to pass in the life of churches—when a vital, vibrant religious tradition becomes a "dead sect, having the form of religion without the power." It has happened before and it can happen again. It can happen to any branch of the Christian Church; perhaps even to the entire tradition. Can we lift any guarantee against it? Yes—but every man and every church will need to put a hand to the standard. The Church can be militant only if its members are willing that it should be militant and are ready to pay the price of militancy. Most churchmen want the Church to be concerned with the whole range of personal problems that invade the lives of men. But are we equally insistent that she be concerned with such problems as peace and war, freedom and tyranny, justice and injustice, brotherhood and intolerance in our social order? Are we prepared to march like the "Fighting Angels" of our tradition in unbroken fellowship on these issues? Or will we look like Matthew Arnold's "The world's poor routed leavings" struggling uncertainly toward a goal we are fearful of reaching?

The answers to questions like these are determined by the insight and resolution of churches like ours and people like us. Once let the awful responsibility of this fateful fact fall squarely upon us, we shall not find it difficult to fall upon our knees in prayer. And we may want to take a cheerful line from Charles Dickens' *Christmas Carol* and make it a solemn prayer of preparation: "God bless us everyone."

2 The Message of the Church:
Tongues of Fire

SCRIPTURE LESSON

And when the day of Pentecost was fully come, they were all with one accord in one place.

And suddenly there came a sound from heaven as of a rushing mighty wind, and it filled all the house where they were sitting.

And there appeared unto them cloven tongues like as of fire, and it sat upon each of them.

And they were all filled with the Holy Ghost, and began to speak with other tongues, as the Spirit gave them utterance.

And there were dwelling at Jerusalem Jews, devout men, out of every nation under heaven.

Now when this was noised abroad, the multitude came together, and were confounded, because that every man heard them speak in his own language.

And they were all amazed and marvelled, saying one to another, Behold, are not all these which speak Galileans?

And how hear we every man in our own tongue, wherein we were born?

Parthians, and Medes, and Elamites, and the dwellers in Mesopotamia, and in Judaea, and Cappadocia, in Pontus, and Asia,

Phrygia, and Pamphylia, in Egypt, and in the parts of Libya about Cyrene, and strangers of Rome, Jews and proselytes,

Cretes and Arabians, we do hear them speak in our tongues the wonderful works of God.

30

And they were all amazed, and were in doubt, saying one to another, What meaneth this?

THE ACTS 2:1–12

I

DR. EDWIN FROST, for many years head of Yerkes Ob-
servatory, is justly known as one of the great astronomers
of our day. I once heard him, in the course of a public lecture
on astronomy, give a graphic description of how new universes
have been formed by the explosion of hitherto stable stars. He
told of the time he and some of his colleagues caught such an
explosion on their photographic plates.

As I recall the story, they had formed an expedition to some
point in the west for the express purpose of making some careful photographic studies of certain sections of the solar system.
They trained their camera on the desired area and took a
series of pictures over several weeks, as the weather permitted.
As they studied the plates they noticed a spot of light in the
lower left-hand corner growing brighter and brighter on each
succeeding plate until, at the end of their studies, he was able
to announce to the world: "A new universe has been created."

As I listened to Dr. Frost tell this fascinating story, I found
myself thinking: "How like that are the origins of great religions!" They, too, seem to burst with explosive force out of
the interior of apparently stable institutions and social orders.
After a period of seething turbulence, they settle down to the
long task of creating new institutions and a new social order.
When they reach maturity they actually have brought into being the outline of these new creations. Their explosions never
reach maximum brilliance and power all at once. They, like the
spot of light on the astronomer's plates, begin in a small, almost
unnoticed, way but grow rapidly larger and more brilliant until

the historian can say, "A new faith, a new church, a new way of life has been created."

This sort of event has taken place not once but many times in the life of the Christian Church. In every case, the "explosion" is simply the Church Militant, the Church bent on redeeming the world in the name and for the sake of Jesus Christ, coming to life again, throwing off her lethargy, clarifying her message and embarking once more on her mission. For message and mission go hand in hand in vital religion. Belief and action are never separated from each other in the great moments and in the great men of Christian history. To believe something meant to do something—so far as they were concerned. They took literally the scriptural word: "Be ye doers of the word, not hearers only." Small wonder, then, they seemed literally to erupt in the life of their time, challenging and markedly modifying the old and seeking to build something new.

Let leaders of the Church who try to freeze the forms of faith as they now are, and friends inside the Church who think her primarily a place for quiet retreat from the world, and critics outside the Church who think her paralyzed by a kind of pious inertia, pause soberly before this well-established historical fact! The more carefully we study several of these "explosions" in Christian history, the better prepared we will be both to understand the extraordinary vitality of the Christian tradition and to expect new things to burst out of its powerful spiritual heart.

II

We saw in our first study in swift panorama how Christian pioneers went to the ends of the earth with the gospel. I propose that we now center our attention in the message itself. For, in every case, a message takes possession of men, building them into a communion, making missionaries of them, and sending them forth on their mission, *new men intent on building a new world*.

Suppose someone had confronted the religious leaders in Jerusalem and the civil leaders in Rome about the year A. D. 27 and said, "There is a young teacher in Galilee who has around him a handful of followers. This movement will soon become the most powerful religious force in the Roman Empire and it will go on to become the great faith of continents as yet undiscovered and millions upon millions of peoples all over the face of the earth." It is understandable that these leaders would have charged such a prophecy off as lunacy. Yet—as we well know—the prophecy itself would have been true enough.

There is no reason to suppose that anyone outside the Christian group itself in those early days had any inkling of the tremendous role it was destined to play in human history. It was—at most—the pinpoint of light in the lower left-hand corner of the photographic plate of that period. Yet it grew with a rapidity and a brilliance that causes historians to this day to shake their heads in incredulity! And the more we know about what went on in those early centuries the more amazing and providential it all seems!

The Christian faith came as a spot of light in the darkness that had settled over the first century. Canon Charles Raven has said of it, "Christianity was born into a world where man's confidence in himself was about played out." The tremendous vigor of Judaism had lapsed into an almost apathetic wait for the Messiah. Thoughtful Greeks might treasure the idea of Plato's *Republic* and dream of the "dear dead days" of earlier glory but they knew how utterly impossible it was to recapture the glory of the days of Pericles, much less build Plato's republic. While they might fret under the rigors of Roman rule, it had put an end to civil strife and the legions kept back the barbarian hordes that were moving about so restlessly to the north. The deep-lying drive that had lifted Greece to a pinnacle of civilization seldom equaled and never surpassed had simply run out of power.

Thoughtful Romans were beginning to lose their optimism about the future. The hard battles that had to be fought almost continuously all along the borders of the Empire plus the ceaseless struggle for control of government and the threat of civil war pointed to an eventual end of *Pax Romana*. While nearly three hundred years would elapse before Rome actually lost her power, thoughtful Romans heard intimations of it from afar.

Ordinary people in that early day lived a harried and anxious life with war, slavery and oppression adding up to a great deal of stark misery. Although their lot was probably no worse than in preceding centuries, a profound spiritual restlessness was abroad. Hope and joy were scarce quantities. Men sought them everywhere. When bread and circuses failed to produce them, people embraced any one of several religious cults that promised them both here and hereafter. Christianity burst out in that world with the force of an interstellar explosion. It came with a shout of confident joy and radiant hope into this atmosphere of deepening gloom and despair. Jesus came teaching and preaching the good news of the Kingdom of God, and, small wonder, "the common people heard him gladly." While the religious leaders of his people preferred to "wait for another," the sheep that were without a shepherd knew his voice and hailed him as the Son of God.

Swinburne could call Jesus a "Pale Galilean" but Will Durant comes much closer to describing his effect in history when he calls him "the greatest revolutionist of all time." Not, surely, in the sense of the barricades which we so frequently associate with revolution, but in the deeper and more fundamental sense of revolutionary goals, values and commitments.

Even when he and his followers seemed defeated by the civil and religious authorities, the light of the new movement kept increasing in brilliance. Luke, the writer of the Gospel of Luke and the book of Acts, never hit on a happier metaphor than in his description of Pentecost: the disciples "were all together in one place. And suddenly a sound came from heaven like the rush of a mighty wind, and it filled all the house where they were sitting. And there appeared to them tongues as of fire, distributed and resting on each one of them. And they were all filled with the Holy Spirit. . . ." (r.s.v.). The result we well know: they went everywhere preaching and teaching the Gospel.

The militant message of these inspired men was simplicity itself: "For God so loved the world that he gave his only Son, that whoever believes in him should not perish but have eternal life" (r.s.v.). God loves man; his love is perfectly revealed in Jesus Christ; through faith in Jesus Christ, man—any man—is caught up in and transformed by the love of God; in Christ we find new life, become new creatures: these are the tongues of fire that brought light into the darkened corners of human existence. This message did not challenge men to believe in God and there let the matter rest. It challenged them both to believe that God in Christ was working a mighty work of transformation in human life and to become themselves co-workers together with God in this work.

What a difference that message made to the men who heard it! So, far from accepting the desperate status of being "atoms in a void" as certain of their philosophers had urged, they were invited to become the sons and colleagues of the living God! Read Marcus Aurelius' *Meditations,* on the one hand, and Paul's *Letters,* on the other, and you will find yourself in two different worlds, spiritually speaking. Marcus Aurelius, Roman emperor and gifted thinker, could find no reason for joy and hope as he went the rounds of daily duty. Here is how he felt about it: "As it happens to thee in the amphitheatre and such places, that the continual sight of the same thing and the uniformity make the spectacle wearisome, so it is with the whole of life; for all things above, below, are the same and from the same. How long then?" Contrast that with Paul's shout of confident joy to the Romans: "For I am sure that neither death, nor life, nor angels, nor principalities, nor things present, nor things to come, nor powers, nor height, nor depth, nor anything else in all creation, will be able to separate us from the love of God in Christ Jesus our Lord" (R.S.V.).

Professor Whitney J. Oates has rightly called Marcus Aurelius' *Meditation* "one of the saddest and most moving books in all of literature." Paul's letters are heralds of a new and glorious day. These early apostles would have no trouble understanding Vachel Lindsay's lines:

> This is our faith tremendous
> Our wild hope, who shall scorn,—
> That in the name of Jesus
> The world shall be reborn! [1]

And it was! These early recipients of the militant message of the Christian faith agreed that love—the love of God—has the last word in life, if we will but let it; that we ought to love one another and show that love in deeds of mutual service and a life of unbroken fellowship with one another; that we ought to regard ourselves as messengers of this love of God both by our lips and in our common life. This they believed. This they preached. This they wrote.

And, lest we think it all added up to one grand spree of uncriticized, undisciplined, and, perhaps, quite useless emotionalism, *consider what they did—these men of the message!*

[1] "Foreign Missions," from *Collected Poems*, p. 338. Reprinted by permission of the Macmillan Company.

To begin with, they became new persons themselves. Saul the persecutor became Paul the apostle. Mary Magdalene the prostitute became, according to legend, the epitome of tender, kindly virtue. Fearful disciples became fearless preachers of the word. Dissatisfied philosophers like Clement of Alexandria became passionate believers and teachers of the new faith. Wherever this militant message went, a kind of moral and spiritual ground swell seemed to shake the whole structure of personal life, and men felt in it the call to a new life.

These men of the message were not content to try to stand alone, much less keep it to themselves. They created groups of believers wherever they went. And in these groups the foundations of social revolution were laid: masters and slaves were equal and equally free in the sight of God and each other; the rich shared with the poor; the well cared for the sick, the widows and the orphans. The faith of all was fanned to a new intensity. Every member of the group became a missionary to friends, neighbors and whomever he met.

Outstanding leaders, like Paul, Peter, Apollos, were sent from one great city to another to present the message with tongues of fire! These men with a message became a group with a mission —the mission of bringing all men, regardless of race, nationality or status in life, into a fellowship with Christ and with those who believed in him. They threw bridges over gaps between and among men and cultures that hitherto had seemed unbridgeable: between Jew and Gentile; between barbarian and Greek; between slave and Roman.

They could do this because the message that made them march was for all men. It arose from the heart of one of Israel's fondest hopes and it spoke, and continues to speak, to the needy heart of men everywhere. There simply are no flaws in the fine universality of that message: "For God so loved the world [the whole world] that he gave his only Son, that whoever [no matter who] believes in him should not perish but have eternal life." Men in every sort and condition of life upon hearing it have exclaimed, "That means me!"

Groups of Christians sprang up with such amazing rapidity all over the Roman Empire that in three brief centuries the Emperor Constantine not only revoked the imperial policy of persecuting them but actually adopted Christianity as the state religion. Charles Norris Cochrane, after studying the relationship between *Christianity and Classical Culture,* says, quite simply, "The theme of this work is the revolution in thought and action which took place during the first four centuries of the Christian Era." The tiny spot of light grew with such rapidity and brilliance that men could say, "A new universe has been created."

III

The same sort of thing happened again in the Reformation. The world to which the Reformation came was one in which the powerful medieval Church had lost contact with the people. She was so intent on seizing and maintaining the control of economic and political power that she was forgetful of the spiritual hungers of common people. This was bad enough but, worse still, was her merciless dealings with all efforts to satisfy these hungers. For three hundred years before Luther, small groups were springing up all over Europe among common people who hungered for faith and fellowship, and, with few exceptions, the Church was pitiless in her attitude toward them and brutal in her dealings with them.

Many loyal churchmen were sickened by what Professor McNeill has called "the moral bankruptcy of the papal church." And with good cause. The high and holy offices of the church, from bishoprics to the papacy itself, were bargained for and frequently bought and sold. The papacy licensed peddlers to roam the face of Europe selling forgiveness of sins for a sum of money. The gross immorality of the Renaissance popes had made morality a by-word in the church herself. Many a devout Catholic sighed with Gasciogne, "Oh, what good might be done by a good Pope!" A few good Catholics like Savonarola signed and sealed their death warrant by an all-out public assault on the immorality and the corruption of the church.

The Reformation burst on this scene with the force of a stellar explosion. A student of the life of Luther has put it this way: ". . . the teachings of the . . . Reformers broke upon the minds of men with the force of a revelation and wrought upon the old, corrupt church with the impact of a revolution." [2] Here are the central teachings that produced this transformation:

1. God speaks His personal word to each man through the Bible, therefore the Bible ought to be in the hands of and known by every man.

2. Each man both may and must approach God directly and personally—not as an abstract religious idea to be mulled over but as an Awesome Fact to be worshiped, adored and served.

3. The Church of God is not a hierarchy of potentates preening themselves on their prerogatives and powers; it is the fellowship of believers—men and women brought together by the love of God revealed in Jesus Christ and described in Scripture.

These teachings are little more than a restatement in terms of the concrete problems of the sixteenth century of the militant message of the early Church. Yet, in the sixteenth as in the first century, they burst into the lives of men with such power and brilliance that we are able to say, "A new universe was created." A new universe—not just a new idea in the minds of a few—but a new universe was created in the affairs of men. Catholic historians sometimes try to dismiss the Reformation

[2] *Protestantism, a Symposium*, p. 423.

as the tragic event that shattered the unity of Christendom and let loose the devil dogs of nationalism, individualism and materialism on our common life. It is hard to believe that a fiction like this can bring much comfort even to the Catholic mind any longer.

If "the unity of Christendom" means acceptance of and docile acquiescence in the spiritual totalitarianism of the Roman Catholic Church, then the Reformation did shatter it, and shatter it so effectively that never again will human spirits that have tasted freedom accept the indignity of that kind of spiritual enslavement.

As the great churches of the Reformation tradition feel their way toward the unity of the National Council of Protestant Churches in America and the World Council of Churches, they are most jealous of the kind of freedom from ecclesiastical tyranny and freedom for creative Christian fellowship that must be considered among the most luminous results of the Reformation. So long as we walk in that light, we shall be living in the new universe created by and through the Reformation.

John Wesley's *Journal* presents an unusually vivid picture of the Church Militant seeking and finding still another medium of expression in the relatively recent past. The spell of Wesley's account grows out of the simple fact that it is what might be called an on the spot report of the genesis of the Methodist Church. Read it with care and, whether you are a Methodist or not, you will see a small spot of light growing with speed and brilliance until a new world has been created.

I think, in the interests of fairness, I should rely on non-Methodist historians for a description of the world in which Methodism was born. One authority concludes his survey of the social, economic and political situation with this terse judgment: "It was an age of bleak tragedy for ordinary people." Historians of the Established Church of England have given equally sharp judgments on prevailing religious conditions. One writer has gone so far as to say that the Church was "never less deserving the name of 'Church' than then." Immorality and frivolity in the laity were matched by those of the clergy. The people, once more, were as sheep without a shepherd. Another writer says, "The darkest period in the religious annals of England was that prior to the preaching of Whitefield and the two Wesleys." [3]

What message did Methodism bring like a light in this darkness? Bishop Francis J. McConnell expresses it in a single sentence: *"What Wesley taught was the worth of man in the eyes of God."* This simple, searching message opened the eyes of ordinary people to God's love for them as revealed in Scripture, particularly the New Testament; it called them to love God utterly and to live in humble obedience to Him; it led them to study His Word and share their experiences of His love and power. Here, again, we have a restatement in terms of the eighteenth century of the militant message: "For God so loved the world that he gave his only Son, that whoever believes in him should not perish but have eternal life." Wesley and his tireless preachers were men with a message, and they went everywhere with it. As they went their rounds the lights of hope and joy began to come up, as it were, in the lives of people everywhere.

Before Wesley died over seventy thousand adults professed membership in the Methodist societies of England. A reform movement within the Established Church was well under way. Social reforms had a new, powerful spiritual ally. An eminent scholar has given it as his opinion that the Methodist movement was a powerful factor in averting a parallel to the French Revolution in England. Be that as it may, we know that ordinary people found a new lease on the spiritual energies for life

[3] Quoted by Buckley, *The Methodist Church,* p. 60.

through it. Coal miners, factory workers, sailors and farmers
walked with new dignity. It is no accident that some of the
most effective leaders in the Trades Union Movement in England today are local preachers in the Methodist Church.

In America the militant message of the Christian faith as
proclaimed by the circuit riding preachers of the Methodist
Church continued to exalt the worth of man in the eyes of God.
It was as fluid and as urgent as life itself. It was preached by
men who believed it could redeem life and usher in the Kingdom of God. They knew of no person or problem that lay
beyond its reach. It was the yardstick with which they measured
the usefulness of the institution and the organization of the
Church itself. These are means to an end—that end is the
proclamation of the Gospel. And what are the results in the
common life of the United States of this elevation of the worth
of man in the sight of God? No man can hope to compile a
complete list of them, let alone measure their worth. But here
are some that bear eloquent witness to the fact that message
and mission, faith and action continue, as of old, to go hand in
hand:

1. The Methodist Church has had a major responsibility in
the creation, and now has some responsibility for the direction
and support of, 150 colleges and universities. Included in this
number are nine of the major universities of the country: Duke,
Emory, Southern Methodist, Northwestern, Boston, American,
Syracuse, Denver, and Southern California. When we say we
believe in the worth of man in the sight of God we interpret it
to mean training our youth to have disciplined, dependable
minds with which to think and work.

2. The Methodist Church has been instrumental in the building and management of seventy-one of the major hospitals of
this country. We have 178 orphanages and homes for the aged
among the many institutions which interpret in terms of con-

crete human problems our faith in the worth of man in the sight of God.

3. The Methodist Church maintains 40,472 churches and provides 25,000 ministers for their guidance. The Methodist Church in the United States now has a membership of nearly 10,000,000 persons. I mention these facts not by way of boasting but in order to explain why there always falls upon us as a Church a heavy yet proportionate responsibility for every cause and plan that looks toward the furtherance of the worth of man in the sight of God. But we need not fear nor should we shrink from that responsibility. We can do it, and do it as it ought to be done if we do not lose either our faith in our message or in ourselves as ones responsible for its proclamation.

When I find myself doubting whether the Methodist Church can measure up to the responsibilities that, clearly, are ours as a Church, I like to recall the words of a prominent Baptist layman. "What I like most about you Methodists is this: When you make up your mind to do something you turn heaven and earth until you get it done." I do not know about "turning heaven," but I do know we stand in a long and honorable tradition of men who have felt called of God to "turn earth" until, in the grace of God, His Kingdom comes.

A friend of mine once said, "What a miracle it is that the God of the universe can use even me!" And it is or should be a profoundly disturbing and moving thought to all that the Pentecostal power is ready to descend as tongues of fire upon the head of every confessing Christian person and church—if we are willing that it should. But let us not ask for it unless we are ready for it. If we know all the answers, we do not need it. If we are satisfied with the way things are going in the human family, we would only be embarrassed by it.

But if we are ready to move away from the crippled, distorted half-lives that we live and lay hold on life abundant; if we are ready to move away from "the giant agony of mankind" toward "the peace that passeth all understanding"; if we are ready personally and in company with one another, to preach to every man in his own tongue the gospel of the love of God as revealed in Jesus Christ, then, for God's sake, let Pentecostal fires descend upon our heads and Pentecostal power take possession of our lives.

3 The Book of the Church:
The Book of Life

If there be therefore any consolation in Christ, if any comfort of love, if any fellowship of the Spirit, if any bowels and mercies,

Fulfil ye my joy, that ye be likeminded, having the same love, being of one accord, of one mind.

Let nothing be done through strife or vainglory; but in lowliness of mind let each esteem other better than themselves.

Look not every man on his own things, but every man also on the things of others.

Let this mind be in you, which was also in Christ Jesus:

Who, being in the form of God, thought it not robbery to be equal with God:

But made himself of no reputation, and took upon him the form of a servant, and was made in the likeness of men:

And being found in fashion as a man, he humbled himself, and became obedient unto death, even the death of the cross.

Wherefore God also hath highly exalted him, and given him a name which is above every name:

That at the name of Jesus every knee should bow, of things in heaven, and things in earth, and things under the earth;

And that every tongue should confess that Jesus Christ is Lord, to the glory of God the Father.

PHILIPPIANS 2:1–11

I

IN THE fall of 1950 a laymen's movement known as Religion in American Life hit the headlines of many of our newspapers and periodicals. As its name implies, its intention is to awaken people to the contemporary value of our religious heritage. *The Saturday Evening Post* devoted an editorial to the effort, giving it the title, "If People Ever Required Religious Faith, It's Now." The editorial asserts, "A major tragedy of our day is the drift of our country, particularly in intellectual and scientific circles, away from the basic religious concepts which bind men of all ages and races together."

This, I am sure, is essentially a true charge, but the tragedy takes in more territory than the writer infers. Intellectual and scientific circles are guilty, to be sure, but so are labor and management; so are newspapers and periodicals; so are the political and civil leaders of our common life. We are all participants, whether consciously or not, whether willingly or not, in the spiritual tragedy of having ignored, or neglected, or distorted, or disowned some of the most important emphases of our religious heritage.

And, what is more, we are discovering, like Jacob of old, that it is easier, far easier, to lose a spiritual heritage than it is to regain it again—especially in a time of great stress. We know to our sorrow how unconsciously we can inherit a great religious tradition, and let it slip away so completely that there is little left but patterns of words and institutions hollowed of meaning to pass on to our children. Small wonder, then, that we and our children feel totally unprepared and wholly inadequate for the days of testing when they come demanding, as they always do, men of granite character.

The Church Militant is no stranger to people in our plight. She is acquainted with earlier generations that were as badly lost as we now seem to be. She has faced and fed faith-hungry people before, and she can do it again. For two thousand years now, she has been offering men like us a Book—the Book of books—and bids us feed on it as the Book of Life.

We must guard against the temptation to pass over the phrase "Book of Life" as a mere glorification of the Bible. It is, in fact, as true a description of the origin, contents and results of the Bible as can be found. The Bible has earned the right to be called "The Book of Life": it was struck up and out of real life; it speaks to living people; it seeks validation in life itself. A careful look at the fuller meaning of each of these assertions will help us understand why the Church Militant is forever talking about the Bible, urging people to buy it, to read it, to study it, to use it as "a lamp unto [their] feet, and a light unto [their] path."

II

The Bible was struck up and out of real life—this is the basis of our confidence in it as the Book of Life. Of course, the same thing can be said with some measure of truth about every great book. Homer's *Iliad* and *Odyssey,* Vergil's *Aeneid,* Dante's *Divine Comedy,* Milton's *Paradise Lost,* Hugo's *Les Miserables,* Tolstoy's *War and Peace,* Dostoevski's *Crime and Punishment*— these and a hundred others are great because they are vital. Touch them, and you feel the vibrations of real life. Listen to them, and you hear some of the deep songs of the human heart. Study them, and you discover that you are among people like yourself who are trying to find an answer to problems that are as old as Adam and as new as you are.

The Bible not so much belongs in this company of great books as it is the unparalleled and actually unchallenged leader of them all. Its sheer vitality, its profound affinity with life, its probing understanding of the very foundations of personal and social life—these set it apart among the great books of the world. We shall not wonder at its wisdom in these matters when we see how it came into existence.

It is, as has been so well said, not so much a book as a library. There are sixty-six books in the copy of the Bible that most of us use. Two tremendous tides in human history produced these books—and many more, to be sure. One was the rise, growth and historical fate of the Hebrew people from about 1300 B.C. to the first century A.D. During this period and about this experience what we call the Old Testament was being written. The second tide was the birth and spread of Christianity over the first two hundred years of our era. Thirty-nine of the Biblical books spring from the Hebrew experience; twenty-seven from the Christian. All in all, they span some fifteen hundred years of human experience and, in their actual writing, represent the efforts of more men than we shall ever be able to number and name. A few—a very few—of the sixty-six books, as they stand now, seem to have been written by one person.

What happened to the Book of Job is a fair sample of what happened to every major book in the Bible. It began its career as a simple folk tale which revolved around a patient man named Job whose loyalty to God stood the test of suffering and who was amply rewarded when it was all over. What we now call the prologue and the epilogue of Job was once the whole story.

Several hundred years after this tale had reached its final form, a profound thinker very much doubted the adequacy of its treatment of the meaning of suffering. So he broke it open, so to speak, and inserted between the prologue and the epilogue a long and carefully reasoned discussion of various meanings of suffering. That became the Book of Job—for a while. Then still another thinker—in a much later period—did the same thing.

Editor after editor, copyist after copyist, translator after translator have left their minor marks on the Book of Job which we have in our Bible today.

Occasionally people are dismayed when they first encounter facts like these about the growth of Biblical books. Yet where is there room for dismay in the discovery that this book has stood the test of time, of human experience; that it is the distilled insight of many ages sincerely seeking the way of man in the will of God?

The early folk tale of Job can be duplicated in a dozen different literatures, but the Book of Job as it now stands can be found nowhere else. It is unique, and it is universal in its scope and appeal. Actually we ought to thank God for His wisdom in letting it come to pass this way! That, better than anything else, explains why the Bible is not, and cannot be made, "the prisoner" of any age, is not dated, so to speak, and thereby restricted in its influence to some one age.

What a panorama of life the Bible spreads before the discerning reader! It witnesses and records the agony and the glory of the long march of mankind from limited to unlimited loyalties; from family, to clan, to tribe, to nation, and, finally, to, mankind; from blood-kinship uniting a few to world-fellowship uniting all. It gives us those revealing insights into the growth and spread of the Christian movement from a Palestinian sect of Judaism to a cosmopolitan church with a faith that sought the loyalty of all men.

The Bible is an appallingly contemporary record of, and insight into, man's quest for peace and security. It is not too much to say that it has seen just about everything tried, at least in principle. In its pages dictators like Pharaoh are more numerous than democrats like Nehemiah, to be sure, but the discussion of the pros and cons of both principles of government abounds.

We see nations seeking their security in power and ever more power, by expanding at the expense of neighbor states—and using strangely familiar arguments about it all being for the best. On one of its pages we see great kings concluding alliances that are guaranteed to give peace, and, on the next, we hear the march of armies as the kings fall out with each other. We hear people proud and confident in their power and prosperity either ignore or defame God and, in adversity, moan, "O God, why have you done this to us?"

The Bible gives us as churchmen a sobering description of what happens when we try to build a wall around our righteousness lest it be contaminated by the evils of the world. That is what the Hebrews did when they came back from the exile. Determined to be a Holy People, a Nation of Priests, they built the walls of Jerusalem, swung the gates in place, and tried to keep out the rest of the world while they kept the laws of their fathers.

Soon the great visions of the prophets had faded away, and their children were quarreling over minor points in the law. How could you be concerned about the human family when you had ten thousand little rules about the Sabbath to follow? It was impossible! So the Sabbath becomes all-important and mankind—God's family—secondary! Self-righteousness swallows up righteousness, and the spirit of religion is dead. Later a son of Judaism was to be killed because he said, "The Sabbath was made for man; not man for the Sabbath!"

Here, unfolded in the pages of this book, is the record of the religious genius of the Hebrews, the most gifted people, spiritually speaking, in our historic tradition. Priests, prophets, wise men and poets have shared in its writing. And the beauty and the power of that writing are without equal—that we affirm with confidence. But, just now, I want to center attention in the living experiences which are mirrored in, and interpreted by, these written records.

There are all sorts of experiences of all sorts of people. William Lyon Phelps said of his book, *Human Nature in the Bible,* "Taking the authorized version of the Old Testament as a masterpiece of literature, I undertook to consider it as a revelation of human nature, in the sublimity, baseness, wisdom, folly, courage, cowardice, tragedy, comedy, normalcy, and whimsicality that have ever been characteristic of men and women." Biblical writers are not content merely to hold a mirror up to nature; they are determined to discover what is going on at the heart of what they see. They are obsessed with the divine depths of everything human; they seek to find the uncommon in the common, the spiritual in the material, the motive in the deed, the purpose in the event—in short, God in creation and life. And they come up with one answer after another—many of them admittedly wrong—until they get one that seems to fit, and stands the test of time.

These facts underlie the assertion that the Bible deserves to be called the Book of Life because it was struck up and out of real life.

III

Add to this a second fact—the Bible speaks to living people—and the reason for calling the Bible the "Book of Life" grows stronger. One of the wisest statements attributed to Robert Hutchins, formerly president of the University of Chicago, is his definition of a classic. "A classic is a contemporary in any age." That fits the Bible perfectly. While some of its material, particularly the chronologies, genealogies and laws of sacrifice, is dated and of little more than antiquarian interest, the rest of it is as contemporary as spiritual insight and moral principle always are. It is impossible simply to read it as you do another book—even a great book; you discover that you are reading yourself in the light of it.

For most of us that is a most disturbing experience. Though
Mark Twain lived at a time when Bob Ingersoll and others
had made it the fashion to call attention to the obscurities of
the Bible, he was much too honest a man to let the matter rest
there. He wrote, "I am not nearly as worried about the part
[of the Bible] I don't understand as I am about the part I do
understand." The great words of the Bible are words of life.
Study them—and yourself in the light of them—for a moment,
and you will understand what Mark Twain means.

Life—the fact of the origin and nature of life itself—is the
first of these great words. For the Bible, God is the Lord and
Creator of life. In Him, and in Him alone, life finds an explanation. It is impossible to improve upon the moving account
in Genesis. "And the Lord God formed man of the dust of the
ground, and breathed into his nostrils the breath of life; and
man became a living soul." I do not suppose that Plato ever
saw or heard of this early Hebrew account of creation, but if
he had, I think he would have understood it and accepted its
basic truth at once. In his own account of creation in the
Timaeus he says:

When God was framing the universe, he put intelligence in soul,
and soul in body, that he might be the creator of a work which was
by nature fairest and best. Wherefore . . . we may say that the
world became a living creature truly endowed with soul and intelligence by the providence of God.

"And man became a living soul"—take this Biblical word
about the nature of life seriously and we discover in it our history and our glory. Every man is a child of God: called of God
to a purpose for living in the will of God. Actually, as Paul
saw, he is a laborer together with God in the realization of
God's will for the world.

This is one of the words of life which the Bible speaks to

every man who opens its pages. And it is a profoundly disturbing word. Once you hear it, life—your life—ceases being a private affair and becomes a gift of God; God entrusts it to you and asks that you be a good steward of the trust. No man is unimportant; no man is negligible; no man can safely be treated as the means to another's ends.

Another great Biblical word of life grows quite naturally out of the first one: *life abundant.* God is the sustainer as well as the creator of life. He does not turn his back on it, so to speak, after the act of creation; rather he works steadily with it, seeking its fulfillment or realization. That is why the Bible constantly urges men to "seek ye the Lord" or "seek ye first the kingdom of God." The firm foundation of the abundant life is a conscious and freely chosen loyalty to God and a complete willingness to do His will in and through daily living.

The Bible is a vivid chronicle of the painfully long struggle of man to do the will of God in a full and satisfactory fashion. Jesus described his mission in these words: "I am come that they might have life, and that they might have it more abundantly"; it was his purpose to release the captives, to give sight to the blind, health to the ailing: to put an end to the worship of power and possessions; to heal the enmity and injustice which separate man from man and man from God. He faced, in principle, every problem we face day by day and, in his life and teachings, he suggests an answer that is based squarely on the foundation of his faith, the worship of God as love and the subordination of all else to that. This, he said, is the nature of, the way to, the realization of the life abundant he came to preach and to give men.

The third great word of life spoken to us by this Book of Life lifts us to the pinnacle of human hope: *life eternal.* The earlier books in the Bible lay little or no emphasis on this word. Some of them seem actually to know nothing about it. Hundreds of years of the deepening of religious insight through tragic experiences and the guidance of the poets and prophets stretch between Job's lament and Jesus' confidence. Job simply accepted as bitterly inevitable the fact that in death he was going to "a land of darkness, as darkness itself; and of the shadow of death, without any order, and where the light is as darkness."

Jesus could say of his disciples: "And this is eternal life, that they know thee the only true God, and Jesus Christ whom thou hast sent" (R.S.V.), and on the cross could say, "Into thy hands I commend my spirit."

The first book in the Bible pictures God creating the earth and the last shows Him re-creating it as the New Jerusalem. That is why we speak of Him as Creator, Sustainer and Redeemer of the world. The idea of the New Jerusalem cannot be charged off as simply a promise of "pie in the sky by and by." It carries a far deeper and truer meaning than that. It is a vision of the triumph of God's will on earth—when His will will be done throughout the universe.

Who among us can regard words like these as relics of a dead faith: *Life, life abundant, life eternal?* They are as fresh, as vital, as vibrant with meaning today as when first uttered to man. They are not prisoners of any age, or book, or writer; they belong to all men and all ages because they are God's way of speaking to His children.

But they are disturbing words—that fact about them cannot be overemphasized. You do not hear them and continue as you are. If you continue as you are, you have not heard them, being like those of Jesus' hearers who "having ears hear not." There is a spiritual power and momentum in these words that keeps life alive; keeps it creative, dynamic, restlessly seeking the higher levels of the will of God. The judgment they carry is a judgment of death only to those who will not hear; it is a judgment of life to those who hear and seek Him "with all their hearts."

IV

A final reason for hailing the Bible "the Book of Life" is found in the fact that *it seeks its verification in the only place where religion can be proved or disproved, namely, in life itself.* It is at this point that religion goes beyond philosophy, goes beyond a way of thinking about life, and becomes a way of living.

It never occurs to Biblical writers to try to separate religion and life; they simply assume that the two are inseparable. Religion interprets the meaning of life, and life tests the truth of religion's interpretation. It is fair to say that the Bible is pragmatic in the deepest sense of that term. The writer of II Isaiah was pragmatic when he invited his people, "Incline your ear, and come unto me: hear, and your soul shall live." Jesus was pragmatic when he said, "By their fruits ye shall know them." And further, when he spoke of those who say, "Lord, Lord," yet who do not do His will. Paul was pragmatic when he told the Galatians what kind of results the Christian faith should produce in their daily lives: "love, joy, peace, patience, gentleness, goodness, faith, meekness, temperance."

The Bible is always confident of the essential validity of its recommendations for living. Priest and prophet might disagree on how properly to worship God but never upon whether there was a God or whether He should be worshiped. Their confidence was in God, and this was the vantage point from which they attempted to understand history and human life.

Historians tell us that the ancient Hebrews did a pretty good job of it, too. Dr. Herbert Butterfield, professor of modern history at the University of Cambridge, gives his highest praise to the Biblical approach to history. He calls attention to the uncanny accuracy of prophetic judgments on historical events. He attributes it to the fact that their faith in God enabled them to see the fleeting events of their time in the longer and truer perspective of eternity. The prophets were continually laying their judgments on the line, in public gaze, and, usually, in the face of loud public disapproval. They awaited the verification of their faith in the events of life and history, and they awaited the decision with equanimity of mind and spirit because their trust was in God, and they knew He could be depended upon. This, manifestly, is the unavoidable final step in religion, according to the Bible.

It is not enough to possess a belief in God; we must be possessed and transformed by it. If your religion does not try to make a profound difference in you—in your attitudes, your values, your plans, your relationships—it is not worth the time it takes. I do not know where you got it, but I do know one place where you did not get it: in this Book of Life and Faith and Works we call the Bible. For this is a book of naked spiritual power aimed at the transformation of the world, not one of kittenish contentment aimed at the enjoyment of it.

Bishop Francis J. McConnell in *Public Opinion and Theology* underscores this fact when he calls the Bible the book of rebellion and freedom. "As long as tyranny is possible in public opinion the Bible will remain the classic volume for the defiance of the free spirit toward tyranny." If the Bible can do that, who among us will stand up and call the knowledge of it negligible and unimportant?

In 1933 the British Bible Society summed up one of the greatest spiritual weaknesses of our day in these cutting words: "The English Bible is today neglected by great masses of people. They perceive no beauty in its literature, no guidance in its teachings, no power in its message." It ought to be apparent to all that we cannot afford that kind of weakness these days.

Too much is at stake for all of us knowingly to tolerate so serious a lack in our spiritual defenses. I would not give the impression that the Bible is a cure-all, and that all we need to do to right the wrongs of our day is to read and study the Bible. But I do want to say with greatest possible emphasis that this is fundamental to every true and ultimately valuable thing we can do.

Arthur E. Holt once spelled out in unforgettable terms the concrete results of telling Bible stories to our children:

They will recognize the supremacy of God over the conscience of men. They will know that this God has sought spiritual maturity on the part of his children, that he is ever seeking to kep alive in them the principle of consent. They will know that there are no preferred classes or races in the community of the spirit. They will demand a social order of which this is also true. They will hold their property for the glory of God and not for personal glory and will demand that the gains of a commonwealth shall be shared gains. . . . They will demand the right to criticize the state and will grow up to understand that freedom of worship and freedom of discussion are necessary thereto.[1]

If the Church Militant proposes seriously to pursue her historic task of being a fit instrument in the hands of God for the redemption of this world from sin, she will fall to this task without delay and with tireless zeal. And she will want to do it in the homes of her people, in her schools, and in her church. She will encourage her people to exalt, to read and to study this Book with such faithfulness and discernment that its great teachings and its even greater life become a strong part of their common life.

There is no surer way of preparing ourselves and our children for creative, courageous, hopeful living in the stern days just ahead.

[1] *Christian Roots,* pp. 54–55.

4 The People of the Church:
New Creatures in Christ

There was a man of the Pharisees, named Nicodemus, a ruler of the Jews:

The same came to Jesus by night, and said unto him, Rabbi, we know that thou art a teacher come from God: for no man can do these miracles that thou doest, except God be with him.

Jesus answered and said unto him, Verily, verily, I say unto thee, Except a man be born again, he cannot see the kingdom of God.

Nicodemus saith unto him, How can a man be born when he is old? can he enter the second time into his mother's womb, and be born?

Jesus answered, Verily, verily, I say unto thee, Except a man be born of water and of the Spirit, he cannot enter into the kingdom of God.

That which is born of the flesh is flesh; and that which is born of the Spirit is spirit.

Marvel not that I said unto thee, Ye must be born again.

The wind bloweth where it listeth, and thou hearest the sound so is every one that is born of the Spirit.

Nicodemus answered and said unto him, How can these things be?

Jesus answered and said unto him, Art thou a master of Israel, and knowest not these things?

St. John 3:1–10

I

WE HAVE been told by a wise student of history that one of the most dangerous characteristics of a civilization in trouble is the temptation to "rest on one's oars," to let well enough alone. In this mood we try to limit our sense of responsibility for the whole of which we are a part by concentrating upon our past: our traditions, our heritage, our way of life, our needs and our future. When this sort of spiritual retrenchment gets under way in a civilization, the first casualty is the degree of community and co-operation that has been won up to that point. We are well aware of the fact—and, I am sure, sobered by it—that we are living in the thick of such a period just now.

It is equally true of churches that, in time of confusion, they tend to withdraw their frontier of responsibility and achieve greater strength and stability by concentrating upon tasks closer at hand. I wish it were not so easy to document this point by current facts. Christian churches are having trouble getting a hearing for a necessary expansion of their work in Japan. The project of a great Christian university there has fallen flat, to date, so far as American interest is concerned. The uncertainty of the future of Christian work in China, Korea, and Asia generally has led some loyal churchmen to question the policy of trying to do anything at all. And so it goes—or threatens to go—in churches in a day of confusion.

Yet, it must be apparent that this attempt to withdraw, to retrench, to disengage the Church in any significant area of present responsibility is as dangerous as it is persistent. To put the criticism of it bluntly: it is unchristian in the exact sense that it contradicts everything we say we stand for in the Christian faith, and it runs counter to the fundamental movements of the Christian tradition in the periods of greatest growth.

Shailer Mathews once ticked off this warning to the Church:
"A faith on the defensive is confessedly senile." And a Church
that seeks to save her life lest she lose it, is, on New Testament authority, sure to lose it.

The Church Militant is the Church on the march, bearing
the standard of the Christ everywhere and to all men. She is
the Church with a purpose—the purpose of God for human life
and history. She is the Church with a program designed to interpret that purpose to the day in which she lives. She is composed of people like us, whose belief in the purpose and program
of the Christian faith leads to aggressive action. She is not a
building, but a fellowship which can meet in and hallow any
building, or, lacking that, the open fields. She is not a liturgical
form, but a fellowship whose worship can express itself through
any and every sort of liturgical form. She is not a tradition, but
a fellowship of people who are inspired by and seek to perpetuate a tradition.

Quite obviously, then, the key word in the Church Militant
is *Fellowship*. And, just as obviously, it is neither a casual nor
an ordinary kind of fellowship. This is the fact immediately
before us now. We need to acquaint ourselves with the special
meanings of that kind of fellowship. We need to get on speaking
terms with the people in it, with what happens to them in and
through it. Finally, we shall want to know where we fit into it
today. I suggest that we walk through certain periods in Christian history and meet the people who were the Church then,
even as we try to be it today.

II

The people in the early Christian groups were "common
folk"—that much is clear on every page of the New Testament as well as in every other scrap of historical evidence we
have.

Read again the straightforward way Paul reassures the Christians in Corinth. Apparently they were flinching under the judgments of the sophisticated, cultured people there. Paul heard of it and wrote these wise and gentle words: "For consider your call, brethren, not many of you were wise according to worldly standards, not many were powerful, not many were of noble birth; but God chose what is foolish in the world to shame the wise, God chose what is low and despised in the world, even things that are not, to bring to nothing things that are, so that no human being might boast in the presence of God" (R.S.V.).

Words like these must have been reassuring not alone to the Christians in Corinth in the first century but to Christians generally for the next two hundred and fifty years. For they were the target of abuse, scorn and harsh judgments from almost every quarter of the Graeco-Roman world. A pagan philosopher, Celsus by name, writing about one hundred years after Paul, gives this sharp summary of the general view of Christians at that time.

He [Celsus] declared that Christianity was the religion of the vulgar and that its founder, the illegitimate son of a poor woman, had wandered to Egypt, where he had learned from the Egyptians the methods of working miracles, and that his disciples were despicable tax-gatherers and sailors with whom he fled from place to place, obtaining a precarious livelihood in a shameful and importunate manner.

What is more, Celsus exclaims, Christians are so immoral as to say:

Everyone . . . who is a sinner, who is devoid of understanding, who is a child, and . . . whoever is unfortunate, him will the kingdom of God receive.[1]

[1] Latourette, *A History of the Expansion of Christianity*, I, 132 ff.

Gibbon, bitterly contemplating the decline and fall of the
Roman Empire, gives the Christians the back of his hand in
this violent, if classic, judgment: "Christians were almost entirely composed of the dregs of the populace, of peasants and
mechanics, of boys and women, of beggars and slaves." Probably the most reliable estimate from the historians is that of
Shirley Jackson Case: Christianity was composed of "the working class and small tradesmen; the majority were slaves, common laborers and people without recognized social status."

Any way you want to look at it, no one joined the early
Christian Church for social or economic or political reasons:
It made its way most rapidly in the lowest social stratum of
that day. Yet it could not be confined to that group. It burst
upward and outward early and with amazing rapidity. Soon
after the learned Celsus attacked Christianity, equally learned
men like Clement of Alexandria and Origen rose to the defense.
Christian thinkers captured school after school in one great
center after another until a literal chain of them girdled the
eastern end of the Mediterranean. Officials might imprison
Peter, Paul and other apostles, but they could not keep the
prisoners from converting their jailers. Before long we hear of
Christians in high office and even in the Imperial household.

The matter, I suspect, can be reduced to some such statement
as this: Christianity grew because it had the common touch.
It gave men a status before God that no human power could
either give or take away. Hence it was prized by kings and
subjects, masters and slaves, rich and poor alike.

The most eloquent evidence of the magic of the common
touch of the early Church is the very language of the New
Testament itself. For centuries Christian scholars were puzzled
by the peculiar kind of Greek used in the New Testament. It
was different from the classical Greek used by Plato and Aristotle. In fact, it was so utterly unlike any other known form

that slightly irreverent scholars sometimes called it "Holy Ghost Greek." The mystery began to lift about seventy years ago with the discovery in the sands of Egypt of literally thousands of records and letters from the first century. All were written in the language used by ordinary people in daily life. Among them were a housekeeper's record of food purchased for slaves; a soldier's letter home asking his parents to send him extra clothing—and countless other items of similar trivial but human nature. The language of these letters and records was "the unstilted language of the people." And it is exactly the same language used in the New Testament. Adolph Deissmann, the scholar who did so much to interpret the meaning of this discovery, says, "The Gospel, because it was the message of God to humanity, could only reveal itself in the simplest of garments." [2] And he puts us professors and theologians with our technical jargon in our place with the observation that Jesus' "words remain in the minds and souls of simple men, who had never been burdered with learned ballast." "In the Gospel simple, great lines join heaven and earth, powerful trumpet sounds arouse the conscience, the everyday facts of human life are the revelation of the Eternal." "Because the Apostles spoke the peoples' languages, the Gospel could go among the masses, could start a mission, and could wander from coast to coast." This New Testament that we handle daily, "this simple book, with its carpenter's and tent-maker's language, was a book for all, and it could resound, unadulterated, to humanity in all centuries, the message of the Gospel which had moved men in a small corner of the Mediterranean world."

We leave the early Church, then, with a fresh awareness of its commonness, its earthiness, its simplicity; with a new appreciation of the power—the sheer power—of ordinary people,

[2] The quotations in this paragraph come from Deissmann, *The New Testament in the Light of Modern Research, passim.*

ordinary language, and ordinary relationships; and, perhaps, with a certain wistfulness because it is so easy for churches to lose the common touch that was the distinctive thing about the early Christian groups.

III

We do well to be wistful about so important a matter. Time after time the Christian Church, intoxicated by dreams of power, wealth and privilege, has lost the common touch, and has been redeemed to usefulness only by recovering it.

There was a time in the latter part of the Middle Ages (about the thirteenth century) when the Imperial Church held title to nearly one-third of the land of Europe, made and un-made emperors and kings, carried on a full-scale war against heretics and heathen, and levied tribute from all Europe. But these facts brought no joy to men like Francis of Assisi and many others who saw the wide gap between the simplicity of the gospel and the pretensions of the Church. All over Europe brotherhood movements sprang up, not so much in protest against the Church as to fill a need in the lives of ordinary people that the Church was neglecting in her pursuit of power. Long before Luther and other reformers had broken with the medieval Church in a big way, hundreds of such simple com-munities were in existence, and they proved to be fertile seed-bed for widespread nurture of the Reformation with its interest in every man for his own and for God's sake. Later, when the great Reformation churches settled into ever-deepening ruts of ecclesiastical complacency (as all did) these selfsame brother-hood movements sprang up again, giving expression to the common touch of the Christian faith.

We Methodists ought to feel the warmth and power of such brotherhood movements in our very chromosomes, for we not only began as one but have never wholly ceased being one. That, I am convinced, is the secret of the growth and power of our Church today.

When we try to estimate our indebtedness as a Church to this or that movement, we face a formidable task. Two acknowledgments can be made, though, almost by common consent. One is to the Church of England who, truly, is our mother Church. She gave us our Articles of Religion, the general pattern of the liturgy we most frequently use, the basic pattern of church government, and our founder—John Wesley—who lived, labored and died a priest of the Church of England. Our debt to this Church, then, is great, but no greater than the one we owe to a whole series of remarkable small group movements outside that or any other historic church pattern. Wesley's own career began as a member of the Holy Club of Oxford University, a small group of devout students who, in seeking the salvation of their own souls, found themselves forced, quite literally, outside themselves, visiting prisons and ministering to unfortunate people everywhere. Bishop McConnell says of Wesley, "He knew more about the inside of jails than any other man in England." This concern for everyone in need became fundamental to Wesley's religious outlook throughout his life.

Still another small group—the Moravians—made their contribution to the Methodist tradition. They were simple, pious, and, for the most part, quite unlettered folk of Central Europe. At first glance they would seem to have little in common with a young priest of the Church of England. But twice they touched him deeply. When he was en route for his brief career as missionary in the colony of Georgia, several families of Moravians were on the same ship. In the midst of a dangerous storm at sea, he felt that his uncontrollable fear contrasted most unfavorably with their quiet faith. They said their prayers with calm confidence; he said his with a note of hysteria in his voice. When the danger was passed, he resolved to look into the matter. Later, when he, like Paul after his experience on the Damascus road, was trying to find his way into a new work, he went to visit their center in Germany. He never failed to be impressed by the way in which all were welcomed and felt at home in their fellowship. Questions of rank, or power, or wealth, or class simply did not emerge. All were one in Christ. Wesley never forgot that; in fact, it loomed larger and larger with the passing years, and as his own work forced him to rely more and more on ordinary people.

Many different accounts have been given for the rapid growth of the Methodist movement. The most convincing one is this: "The outstanding excellence of Methodism on the human side was its virtual discovery of a class or classes of people, whose existence was assumed but not particularly noticed by the more favored groups." [3] Which is to say that although all England was divided into parishes before Wesley began, and, theoretically, the Church was taking care of her sheep, actually she was doing very little with or for the bulk of people then living there. She was doing what the Church is always tempted to do: spend a disproportionate amount of her time on the upper levels of society. She might, and did, baptize, marry and bury the lower classes, but she had no effective way of ministering to them in terms of daily life and work. It was at this point that Methodism entered the picture. Much as early Christianity first moved through the lowest social stratum of the Graeco-Roman world, Methodism moved through the common people of England and America.

One of the most revealing things about those first Methodist societies was their simplicity and democracy. Common, ordinary people felt wanted, needed and warmly welcome. They were invited to share in the spiritual blessings of prayer, study,

[3] McConnell, *John Wesley,* p. 95.

preaching and personal testimony. This was something new in their experience, and they gathered around by the tens of thousands. I do not mean that all of the common people of England heard Wesley gladly. He encountered too many mobs of rough, uncouth commoners for us to think that for one moment. Nor do I mean to give the impression that once a dock worker or coal miner or sailor entered a Methodist society he became a gentle sheep. Wesley had at least as much trouble with his "saints" as did Paul with those in Corinth. His *Journal* resounds with too many a sharp criticism of lazy, ignorant, excitable and superstitious members to permit us to idolize them. But it is true that Wesley, like Paul before him and General Booth after him, took the Gospel to men wherever they were, whoever they were, and by the most useful means he could devise.

In reaching the masses of people, Wesley committed "the unpardonable sin of his time . . . he would not remain true to the attitudes and expectations of his own class." [4] He was both a High Churchman and a Tory by his own statement, yet he broke with both by entering into a relationship of equality with those who were neither. No proper man did that sort of thing. It was not easy for Wesley to do it. In fact, he may have been forced into much of it by his very success. He soon had more groups organized than he could take care of, and he needed help. The only ready source were sincere, enthusiastic laymen who felt the call to preach the gospel. Finally, Wesley began to license them to preach, but not without severe searching of conscience. His brother, Charles, was so indignant about it that he threatened to leave a meeting of a few leaders who were considering this step. John, in true brotherly fashion, merely said, "Give Charles his hat." The wisdom of the decision to permit the abler ones to preach was amply justified by events.

[4] *Ibid.*

An army officer, James Webb by name, was converted under
Wesley's preaching and became a most eloquent preacher in his
own right. Wesley licensed him to preach, and preach he did
wherever his duty sent him. He was influential in founding one
of the first Methodist churches in America. Wesley once said of
him, "He is a man of fire, and the power of God constantly
accompanies his word." John Adams, destined to become the
second President of the United States, described him as "one
of the most eloquent men I ever heard. . . ."

Wesley was not always as fortunate as that in all his lay
preachers, to be sure, but you simply cannot understand the
phenomenal growth of Methodism in England and America
apart from these lay preachers and circuit riders. They were
of the earth, earthy yet luminous with divine light. Coming
from the common people, they knew their hungers and needs
from the inside out. They were living witnesses to the power of
God in human life. It was easier to believe what Nicodemus
found so difficult to grasp when they came down the road. By
their very lives they testified to the love of God for all men
and to His power to transform the life of any man. Thank God,
they kept coming along, generation after generation, from the
ranks of ordinary people.

The Methodist Church shares with all other branches of the
Christian Church this secret of keeping close to common people;
she recruits the overwhelming majority of her leaders from them
all the time. Very few leaders in any of the great Church traditions come from any other source. Like the prophets of ancient
Israel who emerged from the rank and file of the people, thus
feeling and being keenly sensitive to the fears, hopes and faith
of men, the large share of Church leadership has always been
close to the problems of ordinary people. The practice of
celibacy in the priesthood has been of incalculable benefit to the
Roman Catholic Church in this regard. The fact that the great

Protestant churches have their base line of strength in people who are in the lower and middle income and educational brackets has given them the same constant and widespread contact with the moods, impulses and aspirations of common people. Birth, wealth and culture—these commonly accepted marks of aristocracy have been of no consequence in Church leadership. The only mark of aristocracy recognized there is spiritual insight—and this must be attested by its fruits in the lives of ordinary people.

Churches that have emphasized the role of preaching have an added guarantee of being in a close relationship with men. The necessity of phrasing the gospel in terms that get a hearing and win a following has been an unalloyed blessing. Theologians may, indeed must, study and construct systems of thought and expressions of faith, and they are forced to use the exact, if relatively unfamiliar language of their field. The preacher must be at home in these extensive and invaluable efforts, but his task is not that of passing them on, in toto, like a shovel in a conveyor belt. He is an interpreter, a translator of them to people who need the truths they carry. Actually, of course, the acid test of the truth of a theological system is to be found in this complicated act of translation into the parlance of ordinary language and its implementation in the processes of ordinary life.

IV

Looking back over the history of the Christian tradition in general and the Methodist tradition in particular, we make the simple statement of fact: we are a Church of ordinary, common people. The Methodist Church could not be high-brow if she wanted to. Sometimes some of our people and churches are tempted to try, but, somehow, it never seems quite to come off.

One of my closest neighbors and best friends in Baltimore was an Episcopal minister. We soon had quite a friendly rivalry going on the kind of stories we could collect about each other's church. One Monday he burst into our church office laughing so hard he could scarcely talk. I waited patiently, but warily, for him to compose himself. Finally it came out. During his sermon the day before, he was citing the size of various Christian churches, and he made much of the fact that the Methodists then numbered nearly nine million souls. One of his oldest and most devoted members could hardly believe her ears. When the service was over she asked him if she had heard aright. And when he assured her she had, she burst out, in evident distress, "Oh, Dr. Kennan, there must be some well-born people among so many!"

The Church Militant is primarily and always a fellowship where anyone and everyone feels needed, wanted and welcome. If we want the Methodist Church to stand in that tradition— and I am sure we do—there are certain things we can do about it; things that can be done by each one of us, and properly done only when done by all of us. We will see to it that our common life is blessed with simplicity, warmth and freedom.

Simplicity because the gospel itself is simple. "For God so loved the world that he gave his only Son, that whoever believes in him should not perish but have eternal life" (R.S.V.). We shall not want to complicate that by undue emphasis upon theology and liturgy. We shall not want to lose it among the many activities and undertakings of our fellowship. We shall want to exalt it in our life and work because it is our reason for being. No one should ask us to subordinate it to anything else. However strong may be the claim of race, or nation, or way of life upon us, they are decidedly secondary to our main purpose which is to preach Jesus Christ as the way, the truth, and the life to this generation.

We shall want to nurture warmth throughout our common life. Warmth because all real friendship, all vital fellowship is a kind of extension of yourself to others. You reach out a hand of fellowship, in a spirit of warm good will, to everyone else in a truly Christian fellowship. You do not retire within the walls of self and wait for others to seek you out, feeling hurt if they do not; you seek them out or greet them gladly when they approach you. A young man dropped into the evening service of a large city church for the first time and was literally enveloped by the sincere fellowship of the congregation. He wrote home, "It was grand to find so many friends all at once where I didn't know a soul!"

I want to take this opportunity to indicate the wide-open door of full fellowship in the First Methodist Church of Evanston to you who may be considering membership here. I can assure you in the name of this congregation that we want you, we need you, we will welcome you, and we will put you to work! We are a large Church, but not large enough—nor will we be until every living soul in this end of Chicago has been won to a satisfactory relationship with some religious group, not necessarily this one, but some one. The numerical size of a church has nothing whatever to do with the warmth of its fellowship. The largest church in Methodism is also one of the friendliest churches in the world. And I have stepped into churches one-third the size of ours and felt like nothing so much as a bottle of champagne in a bucket of ice cubes. We have a right to be thankful for the warmth there is in our life here, and we have the responsibility to extend it by every means at our disposal.

Freedom—this too is one of the tokens of the Church Militant, the Church we want to bring to expression in our own life. This freedom we need and seek is basically the freedom to love God supremely and to serve Him faithfully all our days. We are participants in a religious tradition, not the slaves of it. We are citizens of this beloved country, yet we hold that citizenship under the judgment of a higher citizenship in the Kingdom of God. We belong to some one general racial line or other, yet we find in the Fatherhood of God an inescapable reason for believing in and working toward the brotherhood of man.

The freedom we seek and need in the Church is the right and the responsibility of every man to meet God face to face as the Captain of his soul, to understand and support one another in this great effort, to present Jesus Christ as the One in whose life and teachings we find our clearest revelation of the will of God for the life of man. And it is the right to do our simple duty: to bear witness to this faith at all times, in all places and to all men.

And if this task seems too big for you, or if it seems futile and irrelevant, *you have the freedom to quit!* If you should feel this way about it, I suggest this epitaph for the person you might have been. It comes from Browning's "Paracelsus":

> I give the fight up: let there be an end,
> A privacy, an obscure nook to me.
> I want to be forgotten even by God.

But most of us will not feel like that. I am confident that the Christian Church will not. Speaking the language of the common man, speaking to the needs and problems of ordinary people, seeking the purposes of God in our common life, she and we who seek to serve her will find ourselves in the tradition of those who call him Lord and Master, who believe that

> He to the lonely soul
> Doth still Himself impart.

We come in the name of One whom the common people heard gladly. We seek to stand in the tradition of ordinary people made extraordinary by their devotion to God. It may be later than we think, but it is never too late for men, for churches, for nations to be born again, to find a new way, a way of life, not death, in His holy will.

5 The Life and Witness of the Church:
A Divine Society

The former treatise have I made, O Theophilus, of all that Jesus began both to do and teach,

Until the day in which he was taken up, after that he through the Holy Ghost had given commandments unto the apostles whom he had chosen:

To whom also he shewed himself alive after his passion by many infallible proofs, being seen of them forty days, and speaking of the things pertaining to the kingdom of God:

And, being assembled together with them, commanded them that they should not depart from Jerusalem, but wait for the promise of the Father, which, saith he, ye have heard of me.

For John truly baptized with water; but ye shall be baptized with the Holy Ghost not many days hence.

When they therefore were come together, they asked of him, saying, Lord, wilt thou at this time restore again the kingdom to Israel?

And he said unto them, It is not for you to know the times or the seasons, which the Father hath put in his own power.

But ye shall receive power, after that the Holy Ghost is come upon you: and ye shall be witnesses unto me both in Jerusalem, and in all Judaea, and in Samaria, and unto the uttermost part of the earth.

And when he had spoken these things, while they beheld, he was taken up; and a cloud received him out of their sight.

And while they looked stedfastly toward heaven as he went up, behold, two men stood by them in white apparel;

Which also said, Ye men of Galilee, why stand ye gazing up into heaven? this same Jesus, which is taken up from you into heaven, shall so come in like manner as ye have seen him go into heaven.

THE ACTS 1:1–11

I

THE city has been called "The graveyard of the church." No cynic coined this phrase. It was a conclusion reluctantly reached by a study made some years ago of one thousand city churches. Since this particular one was published, other studies of the city church have been made and all, to my knowledge, tend toward the same conclusion. As one works his way through such surveys he has no difficulty discovering the major facts that underlie so dismal a conclusion. Actually, they reduce to two: inadequate program and plant; a loss of faith in the Church.

By "inadequate program" the investigators usually meant that the program offered by the church was unable to keep pace with the changing needs of city life. Cities can and do change with bewildering rapidity. No major city and few villages in the United States have stood still over the last twenty-five years. One of our stores here in celebration of Northwestern's centennial has a window display of photographs of Evanston over the last one hundred years. They do more than recall the old days; they tell the story of rapid growth and consequent change in our city's life.

While in Baltimore I had opportunity to study one of our churches that, over a one-hundred-year period, had found itself in four different kinds of city life: suburban; a rooming and apartment house neighborhood; a factory workers' area made up mostly of alien culture groups whose identity shifted about every ten years; a run-down slum area to which people came when they had nowhere else to go and which they left as soon as they could manage it. Under such conditions a church program either changes steadily or the church dies.

By "inadequate plant," the study of city churches meant one that was physically incapable of meeting the needs that people bring to it. Rural churches need one kind of plant, usually the essence of simplicity; city churches need another, usually much more complex and expensive both to build and to maintain. A suburban church facing the needs of a church school for 1,000 people, a young people's program for 600 and a sanctuary for 800 needs one kind of plant. A down town church facing the needs of a school of 250 people, a youth program of 300, and a sanctuary for 1,000 needs a quite different kind of plant. Not many of us would expect a rural plant to work in a city situation or vice versa. Nor would we expect a suburban plant to meet the needs of a down town situation.

Inadequate programs and plants can be remedied—of themselves, they are not necessarily fatal. But couple them—either one of them—with a loss of faith in the church and the death warrant of some church has been signed—signed by the friends of the church—and it will be executed by the changing tides of city life as surely as the sun rises and sets.

Dr. Samuel Kinchloe of the Chicago Theological Seminary insists that loss of faith in the Church underlies all of the major problems confronting city churches. This, he says, is what happens: (1) When confronted by change, churches either resist it or flee in panic before it. (2) Because of the complexity of city life and problems, they get in the habit of dodging the main problems that confront their people. Seeking to preserve themselves from the controversy incident to all vital issues, they suddenly discover that they themselves have become irrelevant. If there is anything deader than an irrelevant Church, it fails to come to mind just now. People will not—and wisely so—long be interested in an institution that does not minister to some deep—even desperate—need in their life.

We pursue our study of the Church Militant in the light of the clear warning that churches can and do have their "time of troubles," that they can and do die. Not necessarily so, but inevitably so where there is a long-sustained and decisive failure in either plant or program or in people's confidence in the Church. Sometimes these failures—particularly in plant—are unavoidable; in which case, the end of the church is entirely honorable. But all too frequently failures are but the just fruits of our own conservatism, indolence and short-sightedness—and against these every church that aspires to live and serve must continually guard. Eternal vigilance and continuing sacrifice are the price of continuous usefulness and creativity in the life of the Church.

The Church Militant is the Church with a message and a mission. It is her duty to proclaim the gospel of the way, the truth, and the life to a world that is perishing for lack of them. The place where she does it is her plant, and the way in which she does it is her program. Plant and program may vary from time to time, but the purpose of the Church is constant. The purpose of the Church is primary; the plant and program are secondary. If the Church is really to be militant, her members must combine unwavering loyalty to purpose with a flexible attitude toward plant and program. And you have the makings of a major tragedy in churchmanship when churchmen become so attached to a particular plant or program that they no longer distinguish between them and the purpose of the Church.

Go anywhere in the history of Christendom, and you will find this truth writ large: The Church in the days of her greatness has never confused purpose with program. Her devotion to her purpose is unlimited and unwavering; her loyalty to any given program is flexible and teachable. The achievement and maintenance of this balance is as necessary as it is difficult. Every individual church must fight and win this battle for itself and within itself if it would continue to be a good steward of its divine purpose. It may encourage us in our task as pastors in every sort of church, to see how others before us have fared in this struggle to keep alive and growing.

II

Early Christianity spread from city to city and village to village in the Graeco-Roman world. Although Jesus and his disciples were essentially artisans, fishermen and peasants in Galilee, the Christian movement took root most deeply and flourished most rapidly in great centers of population. Jerusalem was the home of the disciples of Christ—the pillars of the Church—after Jesus' death. Every major city in the eastern provinces of the Roman Empire was the site of a Christian group before many years had passed. The purpose of the early Church was clear and unequivocal: to proclaim Jesus Christ as the Saviour of the world. Their program was simplicity itself. They met together daily for worship, a meal, and the study of their faith. In addition to these daily meetings, they had much longer gatherings on the Sabbath, patterned after the synagogue services of the Jews. Portions of the Scripture were read and expounded by leaders whom they themselves had selected and ordained. Frequently letters from other Christian groups and leaders were read. They listened to traveling evangelists like Peter, Paul and Silas. They instructed their children in the faith and led converts along the way of deeper understanding and commitment. They took up offerings for the needy and tried to settle the quarrels that arose between and among their members.

Their plants were equally simple. Sometimes they would meet

in one another's homes; sometimes in public parks; sometimes outside the city gates in a quiet place. Occasionally a powerful preacher and teacher like Paul would settle down for an extended stay, as he did in Corinth and Ephesus; then the fellowship would secure a hall in which he would carry on his work. As the membership of the early Church increased, the requirements of both plant and program grew. Instead of beaming their appeal to the lower stratum of society exclusively, they founded schools and encouraged scholars to defend the faith from attack and to secure a hearing for it among the upper classes of the Empire. Except in time of persecution, fugitive meeting places gave way to large buildings—usually of the plainest sort and as utterly devoid of ornamentation as were the synagogues after which they were patterned. Promiscuous leadership—here today and gone tomorrow—was supplanted by stabler resident leadership and government. The churches early became quite suspicious of the motives of exhorters and evangelists who would come around and sponge an easy living off them, using piety as a disguise. In order to control this practice, they passed a rule that I, for one, am glad did not become a permanent part of our heritage: If a man stayed longer than three days, he was not an apostle; he was an impostor and deserved to be cast out! The very existence of this rule gives us a vivid insight into the kind of turmoil which existed in the Church generally at that time. Street-corner preaching, however, was the favorite means of spreading the word, and it was continued with increasing zest and confidence as the Church grew in number and power. Missionaries were sent out in all directions to take the gospel to all men.

Through all this time—over four hundred years—and all these changes, the purpose of the Church never changed: it was to proclaim Jesus Christ as the Saviour of the world, and to proclaim it throughout the world. One form of program after another were tried, modified and abandoned as inadequate. Few if any of them have survived intact to our own time. Yet it was never easy to let go of an inherited way of doing things— even, or should we say especially, in the Church. Most of the major conflicts in the early Church grew out of this fact. Then as now there were loyal churchmen who confused purpose with program.

When Paul, for example, wanted to liberalize the approach of the Church to the gentiles, the pillars in Jerusalem gave grudging consent—and seem to have regretted doing even that much. The Jerusalem wing of the early Church was not at all happy about the mission to the gentiles, especially after it gained so much power. Notwithstanding their lack of enthusiasm for it, the mission to the gentiles rapidly became the Church, and the self-styled "mother church" was faced with the hard choice of either going along or staying behind. She chose to stay behind, and withered away on the vine over the next six hundred years. To this day she continues to be an eloquent symbol of what can happen anywhere.

Paul and other leaders definitely sought to interpret the gospel in the thought and life patterns of the gentile world. Read the letters to the Corinthians if you want to meet some big and many little problems that he helped them face. Other leaders like Clement of Alexandria and Origen introduced the philosophical speculations of the great Greek thinkers—Socrates, Plato and Aristotle—into the Christian Church. In fact, they laid eager hands on truth wherever they found it and caused it to serve the thought and life of the Church. Every good and true thing was grist for their mill. Century after century, this went on until nearly every great fountain of wisdom in the rich heritage of Greece and Rome had been channelled into the river of Christian faith. Though the teaching and preaching program of the Church broadened and deepened her hold on human life as a consequence, her purpose never changed.

One after another, the great art forms of literature, painting, sculpture, architecture and music were pressed into the program of the Church and became invaluable assets in the interpretation and presentation of her purpose. In many ways and periods they have been our most effective preachers and teachers. When I consider how barren our Church would be today without these, I am glad her program was flexible enough to permit their introduction and development.

The evolution of Gothic architecture, to cite but one example, is a testimony to the flexibility of the program of the Christian faith. Gothic took many different forms in every country in Europe and several different forms in France, Germany and England. All these forms are Gothic and all are correct forms. The ultramodern chapel which Frank Lloyd Wright designed for Florida Southern College is as correct as any other form. Few things are more futile than to argue that one form is more correct than another, or that Gothic is more nearly correct than any other architectural form.

For the Church Militant this is the continuing truth: whatever program best interprets her purpose to any given age is the right program for that age; whatever art form leads men into a new appreciation of the meaning of God is correct as long as it does just that. And when it ceases to do that it is not so much incorrect as irrelevant and quite useless. To the Church Militant—the Church that is going places—it is just so much unnecessary baggage.

III

This same combination of steadfastness and flexibility runs throughout the upsurge of Methodism over her entire history. We need to remember this when we get in a mood to try to nail down our destiny to particular patterns of program and ecclesiastical forms. The moment we do that, we will start withering away at the edges because the heart of our mission will have been stilled in death.

When John Wesley sent out his lay preachers he instructed them to go "to the most populous neighborhoods" of England, Ireland and colonial America. Wesley, of course, set the pace, and although he lived to be an old man, he killed off everyone who tried to keep up with him. He seems to have visited every major city in England and Ireland, not once but many times. When he was not there his lay-preachers were, and the work went on without let or hindrance.

The program of these evangelists consisted of three emphases: (1) Preach the gospel; (2) study the Bible; (3) meet together to share experiences of the saving power of God. Wesley wrote voluminously, and his sermons, together with the Bible, constituted the curriculum of the Methodist societies and class meetings.

The plants of early Methodism were equally simple. They were so simple, in fact, that we need to remind ourselves that Wesley never thought of founding a separate church. Methodism, for him, was a movement in the Church of England. That is why the earliest buildings in our Church tradition were plain meeting-places rather than elaborate sanctuaries. Their equipment consisted of four items: a pulpit, a Bible, an altar rail, and benches.

This program and plant seemed eminently fitted to serve the purpose of the new movement. For these early Methodists were men with a mission, and men in a hurry. An English schoolboy was not far wrong when he described that period in this fashion: "Another result of Methodism was that Peace was raging throughout the country."

Looking back on that program, particularly as it developed,

it is easy for us to see real weaknesses that demanded the attention they were to receive by subsequent generations of equally devout men. For one thing, John Wesley never understood the difference between teaching a child and teaching an adult. Sometimes, reading his writings, it seems to me he must have skipped his childhood altogether. He thought the class meeting was as good a way of teaching religion to a child as to an adult! There are times when his blindness on this point reminds me of Jonathan Edwards who took his four-year-old daughter on his knee and tried to make her understand the doctrine of original sin and repeat contritely that she was a worm in the sight of God. If you have a four-year-old around, try that sometime if you want to be really busy!

Another deficiency in early Methodism was the highly emotional nature of the appeal. I am not inclined to be too harsh in this matter because there may have been no other way to get a hearing. John Wesley did not care too much about having hysteria develop in his meetings, and when it did he was more curious about it than encouraged by it. His brother, Charles, positively refused to tolerate it. He announced at the very beginning of one of his services that if anyone felt a seizure coming on, he would be taken forthwith to a back corner of the room for an unspecified kind of treatment. There were no seizures that night.

The rampant emotionalism that attended much of early Methodism offended many otherwise genuinely sympathetic people. Matthew Arnold, for example, was of the opinion that Methodism would not amount to much because it was dominated by a third-rate mind. That judgment, of course, tells us at least as much about Matthew Arnold as it does John Wesley. But it did indicate a needed shift in emphasis from some of the early excesses of the Church. Bishop McConnell is quite just in his observation that one of the problems of early Methodism arose out of the attempt to standardize religious experience. We learned the error of trying to do that; we learned it the hard way; let us hope we learned it well.

Our class meetings gave way to church schools and our circuit riders gave way to the itinerant ministry, and that in turn is gaving way to stabler forms of ministry quite free from limitations of time and travel. The program of religious education in our tradition has undergone a similar development. The actual architecture of a certain city church illustrates this change. When the church was built some seventy-five years ago, the prevalent form of religious education was to undergo the experience of conversion and then share in the class meetings. The plant built by that church conformed to this program. There was the sanctuary with the altar rail and four large rooms for class meetings. Revival services were held once a year, class meetings once a week, and classes for children were sometimes set up in the four corners in the huge sanctuary. History forced changes on both program and plant. The sanctuary and altar rail remain but the four large rooms have been altered. One has been made into small classrooms; one into a little theater; one into a social hall. The fourth has been divided into a lounge and a little chapel. The present program of the church both calls for these rooms and justifies their creation. Yet when the project to make the change was under way, one of the "saints" pleaded with tears in his eyes, and in the spirit of "Woodsman, spare that tree" for the preservation of that sacred building just as it had been built.

Similar changes have been at work in the life of our church here in Evanston for over a century now. In 1836 the first Methodist circuit rider was given this general territory as one point on his charge. The meetings were held in a log schoolhouse some distance west of our present city; later in the second floor of a store; still later in a chapel in one of the first buildings of Northwestern University; finally in a one-room frame structure that was built on the corner where the city library now stands. A much larger church was built on our present location in 1870 and subsequent changes have developed the plant which we have today. Needless to say, these changes in plant were forced into existence by pressures of program and the needs of the growing community and congregation.

Yet I never see a picture of that first building to bear the name of First Church without thinking, and thanking God, that our purpose now is identical with theirs then no matter how widely our plants and programs differ. And as we move into our centennial program in 1954 we shall want to get better and better acquainted with our fathers before us; those mighty men of faith and works of whom we say, "Others have labored and we have entered into the fruits thereof." But we are not merely heirs of their work; we are both responsible creators of our own, and inevitable ancestors in our children's heritage.

IV

Certain great facts loom up each time the panorama of our historic Christian faith passes before our eyes.

First, the secret of the enduring drive of the Christian Church is the conviction that we are a divine society. A society of very human—all too human—people, to be sure, but nonetheless divine in a most exact sense: We are called of God, even as our fathers were, to confront this generation with His will as we see it in Jesus Christ; we are called of God to bring our generation under the judgment of His holy will—to measure ourselves and our works against His intention for us; we are called of God to do this without fear of any man and with love for all— and to keep on the job all our life. The true heart of the Church is the conviction that God was speaking to us when he said, "I have made thee for myself; thou art mine."

The second conclusion is this: We must go about the task of interpreting the Christian faith to this generation with complete freedom to do it in the best way possible. There is such a thing as being openly and honestly indebted to the deeds of our fathers without being bound by them as we face our work. It is spiritual betrayal to forsake the continuing purpose of the Church; it can easily be the sum of good judgment to alter plant and program the better to probe the needs of our day. It is our steady purpose to preach the gospel everywhere—there can be no compromise with that. But how best to do it? Street-corner and open-air preaching—once so effective—are of dubious value today. Radio, television, books, pamphlets and other ways are their equivalents now. We must take the gospel to people where they are and cast it in terms that they understand and keep everlastingly at the task until life is done.

A third conclusion is this: Every churchman is the Church. You are the Church. The Church is not something that exists outside of you: you are an integral part of her and she of you. Someone has said that "a gentleman will never find himself in a situation where he cannot be a gentleman." I would like to make the obvious paraphrase that "a churchman will never find himself in a situation where he cannot be a churchman." Once you accept the purpose of the Church, you are the Church as truly as anyone has ever been or will ever be. Whatever your profession may be, you have but one true vocation: you are a Christian churchman. You are the voice through which the gospel speaks or tries to speak or fails to speak to this generation. You are the conscience through which the gospel cries aloud or fails to cry aloud in protest against the evils of our life and time—and when you cry aloud you do so not in your name but in God's name and for His sake. You are the one through whose life the love of God becomes or fails to become a new fact and factor in a world where hatred and injustice are so prevalent and powerful.

And in the sanctuary of the Church, in the life of every congregation, the separate "yous" of all of us become the "we" of the Church Militant. For we are members one of another, even as Paul said. We belong to and enter into the fellowship of the faithful who through the centuries have been the Church in their day.

Is the age-old purpose of the Christian Church to be a power in the lives of men today? Is the gospel to be proclaimed with power today? Are the great ideals of Love, Mercy and Understanding to be held up by steady hands and steadfast hearts today? The answer rests with us.

6 The Vision of the Church:
The Kingdom of God

SCRIPTURE LESSON

When the Son of man shall come in his glory, and all the holy angels with him, then shall he sit upon the throne of his glory:

And before him shall be gathered all nations: and he shall separate them one from another, as a shepherd divideth his sheep from the goats:

And he shall set the sheep on his right hand, but the goats on the left.

Then shall the King say unto them on his right hand, Come, ye blessed of my Father, inherit the kingdom prepared for you from the foundation of the world:

For I was an hungred, and ye gave me meat: I was thirsty, and ye gave me drink: I was a stranger, and ye took me in:

Naked, and ye clothed me: I was sick, and ye visited me: I was in prison, and ye came unto me.

Then shall the righteous answer him, saying, Lord, when saw we thee an hungred, and fed thee? or thirsty, and gave thee drink?

When saw we thee a stranger, and took thee in? or naked, and clothed thee?

Or when saw we thee sick, or in prison, and came unto thee?

And the King shall answer and say unto them, Verily I say unto you, Inasmuch as ye have done it unto one of the least of these my brethren, ye have done it unto me.

Then shall he say also unto them on the left hand, Depart from me, ye cursed, into everlasting fire, prepared for the devil and his angels:

For I was an hungred, and ye gave me no meat: I was thirsty, and ye gave me no drink:

I was a stranger, and ye took me not in: naked, and ye clothed me not: sick, and in prison, and ye visited me not.

Then shall they also answer him, saying, Lord, when saw we thee an hungred, or athirst, or a stranger, or naked, or sick, or in prison, and did not minister unto thee?

Then shall he answer them, saying, Verily I say unto you, Inasmuch as ye did it not to one of the least of these, ye did it not to me.

And these shall go away into everlasting punishment: but the righteous into life eternal.

ST. MATTHEW 25:31–46

I

TOUCH the Christian Church anywhere in her two-thousand-year career, and you have laid your hands on something in motion. She is not a static entity that can be completely and satisfactorily described in terms of any given here and now; she is a dynamic movement whose rich reality includes not alone what is but also what is to be. Yet her motion is never mere activity; it is an honest effort to reach a goal, and that goal is the Kingdom of God.

This loyalty of the Christian Church to the Kingdom of God, this determination in the heart of the Christian Church to be an instrument in the building of the Kingdom of God, sharpens up one of the most important facts about the Church. And yet, I must say, it is frequently ignored or misunderstood by casual onlookers and secular-minded historians alike.

Mr. John Flynn in his diatribe, *The Road Ahead,* pours scorn on the "Kingdom of God" emphasis in Church thought and life today. Nowhere does he pause to investigate either the history or the meaning of the idea of the Kingdom of God in the Church. Tell him that the Christian Church has no meaning, because she has no mission, apart from the idea of the Kingdom of God, and he will call you a poor misguided idealist and lecture you sternly on the evils of socialism. He is entirely correct in his feeling that the preaching of the Kingdom of God by the Church today is pregnant with social criticism and reform, but he is pathetically wrong in his assumption that socialists and other radicals are to blame for this fact. Criticism and reform are inseparable from the idea of the Kingdom of God—this discovery is coming as hard for many of us today as it did for Jew, Greek, Roman, feudal lord, and dictator in ages gone by.

Mr. Stanley High takes advantage of his "privileged sanctuary" in the *Reader's Digest* to mount his attack on the social radicals in the Church, to weep copious (if not crocodile) tears of sympathy for you laymen whose simple piety is imposed upon by these radicals. He urges you "to throw the rascals out." He counsels you to listen, rather, to some more dependable leaders, and, with becoming modesty and fetching indirection, volunteers his own services.

For all I know he may be a dependable guide, but I cannot tell and will not hazard a guess until I know more about what he means by, and proposes to do about, the Kingdom of God. Is it, as I greatly fear from his fugitive writings, a condition in which the Church is so thoroughly domesticated as to munch contentedly on the hills of special privilege, letting down her milk at the appointed time like every contented cow should? If so, then the long succession of men who for the sake of the Kingdom of God faced without fear and without compromise the kingdoms of this world must be listed high among the world's foolish children.

Nor have secular-minded historians had much better luck understanding the Church than have such publicists as Messrs.

Flynn and High. They too have tried to chronicle the influence of the Church in and on history without taking the trouble to grasp the fundamental meanings of the idea of the Kingdom of God to the Church and in the life of her people.

It is a good axiom for historian and any other student of human behavior to know the purpose, the goal, or the motive of an action in order to understand that action. It is not enough to describe *what* the Church has been and done: You must be able to say *why* she has attempted to do it. The Kingdom of God is the *why* that helps us understand the *what* of Christian life and history. And it is to this task that we address ourselves now.

II

If the Church Militant, the Church on fire with great Christian convictions and determined to bring them to bear upon our life and time, is willing to take seriously her historic faith in the Kingdom of God, she will be making her greatest contribution toward the salvation of our world. For, by lifting up the Kingdom of God and marching under it as under a banner unfurled, she will be correcting a fatal confusion in our ethical thought about ends and means; in addition, she will be pointing and trying to lead the world toward a new goal, one that in an open road to life rather than the blind alley in which we find ourselves groping today.

Much, if not most, of the moral chaos of our time arises from the fact that we are all mixed up about the relationship of ends and means. For a long time now we have believed and acted on the assumption made famous by the Jesuits in the days of the Inquisition that "the end justifies the means." This is the root-philosophy of every dictatorship that has arisen to plague our common life. It underlies the argument so often advanced by some of our economic leaders when they assume that the working man does not know what he wants, so they will have to do his thinking for him and make him like it. Many a churchman has accepted and advocated war as an admittedly evil means toward the good end of freedom, security and peace.

We should have known better if we had paid more attention to our New Testament. For this perennially important document warns us that men cannot gather figs from thistles or good fruits from an evil tree. In direct violation of these warnings, we try to persuade ourselves that evil means can sometimes be made to serve good ends, and when they do, they are justified, if not in the sight of God, then in the sight of men of good will. I can understand it when men who make no pretense of knowing the New Testament get taken in by this kind of reasoning, but I find it more difficult to understand when it comes from confessing churchmen.

Emerson drove to the heart of the matter, scripturally as well as ethically, when he said, "The end is pre-figured in the means." From the very beginning of Christian history, the supreme end of Christian life and work has been the Kingdom of God, which is God's will in history. Without it the Christian gospel is a clarion call to nothing in particular. It is the end, and the only end, plainly pre-figured in the kind of life Jesus recommended to his disciples. The startling ethical principles of the Sermon on the Mount are means aimed at the end of the Kingdom of God and at no other end known to man. We have not yet been able to persuade ourselves or anyone else that we can achieve the Kingdom of God by any other means than those outlined by Jesus of Nazareth.

So it is of utmost importance that we clarify our thinking on the meaning of the Kingdom of God both in our gospels and in terms of our common life today. It is easy enough to stand up and repeat together, "We believe in the Kingdom of God as the divine rule in human society, and in the brotherhood of man under the fatherhood of God." But it is far more difficult to accept this as the goal for our thinking and living. Yet, as I understand the Christian faith, that is our clear responsibility.

III [1]

Both John the Baptist and Jesus of Nazareth began their public life with the announcement of the imminence of the Kingdom of God. There was real confusion among their hearers as to what they meant because several conceptions of the Kingdom were current at the time. "What do you mean by 'the Kingdom'?" was their natural query. That is why the Gospels spend considerable time trying to clarify the meaning of the Kingdom. It would be pleasant to report that they settled on one clear idea, but the truth is far different.

There is no one conception of the meaning of the Kingdom in the Gospels. In fact, the *Dictionary of Christ and the Gospels* concludes its careful survey of the variety of meanings of the Kingdom of God in the New Testament with these words: "From this survey it is readily seen that the term 'Kingdom of God (or Heaven)' in the usage of Jesus is not easy to be defined; that it appears to be an elastic poetic symbol rather than the vehicle of a single, sharply-founded conception." Against the background of this warning, the writer of the survey hazards the judgment that the fundamental thought of the term, Kingdom of God, is something like this: "Where the will of God is done, there the Kingdom of God has come . . . accordingly . . . the fundamental idea of the Kingdom of Heaven is the rule of God." As you work your way through the various studies of the meaning of the Kingdom of God in the New Testament

[1] Most of the material in this section appeared as a portion of the chapter "We Believe in the Kingdom of God" in my book *A Firm Faith for Today*.

you come to the conclusion that among the rich variety of ideas and suggestions about its nature, these three stand out:

1. *The Kingdom is a future material reality.* It will be an earthly Kingdom established by God through a decisive victory over Satan. It will be for those whose lives have undergone moral transformation. Jesus is preparing men for entrance into the Kingdom when God inaugurates it. But man can only be prepared for it. He can neither force its coming nor know when it will come. Like the wise and foolish virgins he will either be ready or unready for it when it comes.

2. *The Kingdom is an existing spiritual reality.* "It consists entirely of the triumph of Righteousness, of the love of God and of our neighbor, and of divine peace in the heart of man." It is always at hand in the exact sense of being a permanent possibility in human life. Man can always step over the threshold if he is willing to become a fit citizen of the new order. Naturally, it will spread from person to person until finally it becomes a new social order, one in which love and community are basic. This means that its growth in human affairs will be slow, like the growth of a mustard tree, or the work of the leaven in the lump. It is to be the earthly beginning of a condition of life that will be perfected in heaven. Jesus is setting men's feet on this pathway by uniting them with God and man in such way that their lives will be transformed. As Dr. Manson writes: "Jesus offers to his nation not a new doctrine of the Kingdom of God but a new conception of God's will which, if received, will bring the goal indicated by the Kingdom of God into measurable, indeed into immediate relation with the lives of men."

3. *The Kingdom is fundamentally eschatological in nature.* Which is to say that it is primarily a matter of "final things," rather than present events. It is something that will happen in the future, at the end of time and history, and it will add up

to the complete transformation of all earthy things. The earth and the sea will be consumed in fire and all men brought to final judgment. The good news of the gospel is to assure men that the Kingdom is at hand, and, in their fellowship with Christ and one another, to give them a foretaste of what it will mean by outlining the meaning of citizenship in it. "Although principally the work of God, it is, in so far as it is a present thing, the work of Christ, for its perfect achievement will only be realized if certain conditions of a moral order are fulfilled."

It has even been suggested by some students that Jesus' own conception of the Kingdom grew with his experience; that he began by regarding it as an imminent earthly Kingdom, later feeling it to be a spiritual reality, and finally accepting the eschatological notion of it. Be that as it may, the plain truth is that a variety of meanings cluster around the concept in the Gospels.

With so much diversity of meaning in both Jewish and early Christian interpretations of the meaning of the Kingdom of God, we shall not be surprised to learn that succeeding Christians have felt free to use any one of them. There can be little doubt that the one most widely used during the history of the Church regards the Kingdom as a world of perfection lying wholly outside, if not beyond the reach of, this world. Heaven has been a synonym for it in everyday thought and speech. The Kingdom is to be the New Jerusalem outlined so graphically in the Book of Revelation. Its appearance in God's own time will herald the end of the world and the return of the Lord Jesus to judge the quick and the dead. When this is done, and the wicked condemned to their punishment, the millennium of peace, wherein God's will prevails on earth, will occur.

A relatively recent conception of the Kingdom pictures it as an ideal world to be fashioned by divinely inspired men out of the materials of this life and world. When men speak of "building the Kingdom" some such image as this invariably and rightly flashes across our mind. This conception is neither mean nor prideful as so many critics have pictured it. It need not be a glorification of man; in fact, it is a glorification of the power of God which re-creates life both personally and socially. The reality of God is as central in this idea of the Kingdom as in the more prevalent one. The reality of man as a responsible creature of God is much more in evidence in the latter notion than in the former.

Much of the discussion about the meaning of the Kingdom of God revolves around the where, when and how of its nature and coming. There is no use pretending that we have conclusive information on such points. So far as the Bible and Christian history are concerned we plainly do not. This, however, does not mean that we are completely in the dark as to the meaning of the Kingdom for human thought and life. On the contrary, some are both indisputable and immeasurably important in our understanding of the Kingdom, which is the goal of Christian thought and life.

It is God's Kingdom. It is not Caesar's, not even man's; it outranks these in every way. No man, no nation, no race will dominate it with its will. Citizens of the Kingdom will be men whose wills are moved by God's will and purpose. To use two clumsy but exact words, the Kingdom of God is both theocentric (centered in God) and theocratic (ruled by God). Humility and obedience alone can open the doors for one to enter the Kingdom. That is why the penitent Publican of Jesus' parable "went down to his house justified," while his proud companion stood outside and alone. Jesus' own humility in the presence of God's will is instructive. For obedience to the will of God is the North Star of his life. That is why he taught unnumbered millions to pray, "Thy kingdom come, thy will be done on earth as it is in heaven." Dr. William Manson is persuaded that the fundamental meaning of the Kingdom of God lies in this area: "A supernatural would arise in whch usurping evil would be judged and removed, and God would be visibly revealed as Saviour of His people. In short, it would be the perfect rule of God."

The Kingdom of God—to come to closer grips with it—is the condition in life when God's will is understood and fulfilled. At once we confront the tragic fact that this condition has never been achieved by anyone, individually or collectively, excepting, always, Jesus Christ. Yet even in him there is the prayer in the Garden which indicates that he found it difficult to be perfectly obedient. The reason for our failure is not hard to state. God made us men and not machines. If we obey Him, it is because we choose to do so. If we disobey Him, it is usually for the same reason.

The Kingdom of God is that condition in which His perfect will for our good is seen, chosen and realized. This, of course, exists only ideally at any given time short of its realization, much as docking at a port exists ideally until it actually is done. But this fulfillment is not forced upon us in spite of ourselves. If it is ever achieved, whether in personal or social living, it will be because people neither better nor wiser than we are seek it with all their hearts, confident that, as God lives, that is their duty and their high privilege.

V

Living as we do, and ministering as we must, in a day when anxiety, fear and hatred loom so large in the thought and heart of mankind, when despair rather than hope seems to be the final posture of the human spirit, we need to renew our belief in and loyalty to the Kingdom of God. Even though we may not be able to put down in logical and theological propositions all that it means, we have the right to be encouraged by what it has meant to our fathers before us as they marched under the banner of the Church Militant. So far as I can interpret the record, belief in and loyalty to the Kingdom of God yields four inner qualities that are inseparable from significant Christian living.

First, there is a sense of mission, of purpose driving every true member of the Church Militant. He is called of God to the task of proclaiming the Kingdom of God. This human mission by man to men begins, continues and ends as a Divine Commission. Once this conviction of purpose gets hold of a person he has an end and goal for living. He knows and finds peace in the simple fact that he knows—where he is going and why he is going there.

A second quality is a sense of fellowship with man and with God. Once grasp the fact that God in Christ was speaking His word of forgiving, redeeming love to all men everywhere, and that we are called of God to be heralds of this gospel, we approach all men on a level of compassion and understanding. Differences of creed, race and nation cease to be important; they may cease to make any difference at all. Welling up within us is the overpowering conviction that we are One in Christ. This is a blessed fellowship, but the Church Militant is not privileged merely to enjoy it. She must seek to win all men to an awareness of it. By life and word, she must pursue this task until the Kingdom comes.

A third quality of life which sustains the Church Militant is a kind of patient, unbreakable courage. That sort of courage will ever be one of the cardinal virtues of significant Christian living. It takes courage to challenge the entrenched powers of Church and State when they trespass on human rights. It takes courage—the courage of a Niemöller or Berggrav—for Christian people living in social orders that are openly hostile to religion to continue to bear their witness. The continued witness of the Orthodox Church in Russia despite relentless pounding with every device of a ruthless government from 1917 to 1939 is likely to become one of the great instances of the sheer courage of the Christian faith. The leaders of the Christian churches in China know that testing times are upon them, but they seem to be ready for them and face them with no thought of weakening. And as we pray God's help for them, we know in our hearts that the prayer is already answered with an answer that will not fail.

A final quality that shines with brilliance in the Church Militant is joy. The frequency with which the admonition to "Rejoice" occurs in letter and in spirit throughout the New Testament, and again in the writings of Christians in difficult days, is most instructive. Mr. Gerald Heard somewhere draws this contrast: The petition "Thy kingdom come" is not so much a shout of joyous expectation as an anxious, fearful whine. From the beginning, Christians have rejoiced in their call to find new life in Christ and to preach this fact as the gospel. There is a radiance about their witness that transcends differences in thought, age and culture. To know Christ was life: a kind of life with him, with God and with man that faced the trials of life and the terrors of death unafraid.

This, then, is the banner we unfurl when we dedicate the Church Militant to the Kingdom of God. For when we say we believe in the Kingdom of God we are making a realistic statement about the nature of the world, the meaning of history, and the character of the good life.

We are saying that life has a purpose, not our purpose, but one in which we can find truly significant purposes. We are saying that living in and by that purpose is both a way of life and strength for pursuing it with a whole heart and mind. We are

saying that this purpose is as truly concerned with the ordering
or salvation of society as with individual life. For the Christian,
then, the Kingdom of God is not a creation of his imagination; rather, he seeks to be a creature of its ultimate and eternal
meaning. To the extent that he is able to do this, the Kingdom
has come. In brief, then, when we say we believe in the Kingdom of God we are putting in a single affirmation a series of
the most important resolutions a person or a people can make.

The Kingdom of God is a life to be lived, a work to be done,
a destiny to be fulfilled. It is a new life—our present life redeemed and renewed by a humble and sincere appreciation of
God's will for life as we see it in Jesus Christ. It is a work to
be done—since the steadiest emphases in the teachings of Jesus
are calls to action, work and duty. It is a destiny to be fulfilled—the achievement of the peace and poise known to those
who find their way in the will of God as seen in Jesus Christ.

We know—and how well we know!—that Jesus was speaking to us when he said, "The kingdom of God is within you."
Within me? Surely that must be written off as Oriental hyper-
bole. He cannot have meant that the supreme end and goal of
Christian thought and life is within me. And yet the evidence
is conclusive that that is precisely what he did mean.

Within each one of us is God's intention for us, God's perfect
will for our life. This is the deepest, the truest and the most
glorious fact about us. It is seeking full and free expression in
our life, but, as our fathers were fond of saying, we have
hindered it. Sometimes consciously and willfully, sometimes unconsciously and accidentally, we have blocked it by passion,
greed, selfishness and every other form of sin. But nothing we
do can snuff out the inner glory of God's perfect will for us.
The Kingdom of God is within you.

It is within our homes, churches, communities and our
world. It is within our relationships, and it carries with it the

intention and the power to overcome all divisions among men. It is God's perfect will for us and it continues to be precisely that even when our personal and communal lives are distorted by the hell of human choices. One of the deepest reasons why we refuse to accept such divisions and conflicts in human life and society is the reality of this intention of God which keeps breaking through to consciousness, revealing, as with a flood of light, the tragedy of our ways and opening up vistas of the perfect way. One of Augustine's truest, and probably his most famous insight is this: "Our hearts are restless until they rest in thee."

As the late William Temple was fond of saying, "The Kingdom of God is the sovereignty of love." This is a singularly acute way of stating an age-old conception of the Kingdom of God. Better than anything else, it drives home the fact that the Kingdom of God is not an other-worldly affair; it belongs to this world in the literal and exact sense that it serves as the ethical standard by which we measure our motives, plans and deeds. By so doing it places upon man the unmistakable stamp of divine worth and eternal destiny, for God not only loves man with a love that outdistances our most far-ranging imaginations, but He trusts man to hear and heed His will for life and history, and to become a co-worker together with Him in the redemption of the world. This conception of the ultimate nature of the universe and human history is the firm foundation for Christian ethics—an ethic, let it be underscored, that aims at nothing less, and can be satisfied with nothing less, than new men, a new order of society, and a new direction for human history.

While convictions like these about the nature and the meaning of the Kingdom of God are not, and cannot be, presented as blueprints for specific and detailed changes to be made throughout society, they will, if and to a degree that they are taken seriously, keep Christian men everlastingly at the task of trying to discover the outline of such blueprints. Only two persons can seriously object to this effort: One who thinks the world cannot be improved, and one who thinks the Kingdom of God is either already here or was not meant to be relevant to human life and history. All other Christians will fall to the task of fulfilling the vision of the Kingdom of God. Until that comes, we will say with William Blake:

> Bring me my bow of burning gold:
> Bring me arrows of desire;
> Bring me my spear: O clouds unfold!
> Bring me my chariot of fire.
>
> I will not cease from mental fight,
> Nor shall my sword sleep in my hand
> Till we have built Jerusalem
> In England's green and pleasant land.

7 What is the Church?

Wherefore laying aside all malice, and all guile, and hypocrisies, and envies, and all evil speakings,

As newborn babes, desire the sincere milk of the word, that ye may grow thereby:

If so be ye have tasted that the Lord is gracious.

To whom coming, as unto a living stone, disallowed indeed of men, but chosen of God, and precious,

Ye also, as lively stones, are built up a spiritual house, an holy priesthood, to offer up spiritual sacrifices, acceptable to God by Jesus Christ.

Wherefore also it is contained in the scripture, Behold, I lay in Sion a chief corner stone, elect, precious: and he that believeth on him shall not be confounded.

Unto you therefore which believe he is precious: but unto them which be disobedient, the stone which the builders disallowed, the same is made the head of the corner,

And a stone of stumbling, and a rock of offence, even to them which stumble at the word, being disobedient: whereunto also they were appointed.

But ye are a chosen generation, a royal priesthood, an holy nation, a peculiar people; that ye should shew forth the praises of him who hath called you out of darkness into his marvellous light:

Which in time past were not a people, but are now the people of God: which had not obtained mercy, but now have obtained mercy.

I PETER 2:1–10

I

FEW institutions have suffered so much at the hands of public opinion as has the Christian Church. This opinion has oscillated, like the swing of a pendulum, between widely separated points. Sometimes the Church has been called useless; other times she has been lauded as man's best hope for a new world. Sometimes she has been pitied; other times, feared and hated; still other times, adored with restrained or fanatical devotion. Sometimes she has been devoid of almost all material possessions and, seemingly, a negligible fact in life and history; other times she has been wealthy, powerful, and obviously a most important fact to be reckoned with.

It was almost yesterday—less than a hundred years ago in fact—when sensitive figures like Leo Tolstoy were writing the Church off as useless. William Watson, an earlier contemporary of ours, dismisses the Church with this quatrain:

> Outwardly splendid as of old—
> Inwardly sparkless, void and cold—
> Her force and fire all spent and gone—
> Like the dead moon, she still shines on.[1]

And Joseph Wood Krutch, writing in the twenties, speaks of the Church as "that great authority against which young people have not so much revolted as by which they have suddenly found themselves no longer impressed."

The pendulum of public opinion is swinging back in our time and has been swinging back over the last decade. Interest in the Church, an honest respect for the Church, belief in the Church's role in life and history, a willingness to share in the

---

[1] "The Church Today" from *The Poems of Sir William Watson 1878–1935*. Reprinted by permission of George G. Harrap & Co., Ltd., and Lady Watson.

life and work of the Church—these, if not at an all-time high, exhibit a noticeable increase. Mr. J. B. Priestley, well-known British writer, is, I suppose, one of those "young people" of the twenties to whom Mr. Krutch refers—one who found himself "no longer impressed" with the Church. Rough as the last thirty years have been on people who tried to maintain a great religious faith, they have been even rougher on those who tried to get along without one. Writing now, Mr. Priestley says,

People like my parents—to use their own matchless phrase—attended places of worship. Now that I see that old phrase with a fresh eye, I also see how astonishing it is. Places of worship. How much we have lost, we of the younger generations, by having no places of worship! Perhaps this new world must remain desolate at heart until it achieves new places of worship. Then the spirit of Man will come home again to the universe. . . . What is certain is that the absence of church or chapel from these young people's lives has vastly increased their sense of detachment and their feeling of loneliness. When I was a boy the chapel played a very important part indeed in the communal life. It was the great focal point, the center, the meeting-place. Something was always happening there. If the chapel had been taken away there would have been an enormous gap, and I fancy not all that gap has been filled. It is possible that the moderns in their labour-saving flats or natty bungalows will not live richly and deeply again, will continue to feel that there is something sterile and faintly desolating in their lives, until some central institution like the old chapel, with the same focusing of interests and the same sense of community, is created once more. And if this new institution can be dedicated to men's profoundest beliefs and emotions, to their conviction that they need not be lost in the universe, then so much the better.[2]

It is perhaps enough to say that our secular, materialistic, pagan age is learning to its amazement, if not chagrin, that the Christian Church is not now and never has been on trial for the right to be considered a vital factor in human life and

[2] *Rain upon Godshill*, pp. 249–50.

history. Someone's on trial, all right, but it has been and continues to be those who think it does not much matter what
the Church thinks or proposes, that it does not much matter
whether the Church lives or dies. They had their chance to
demonstrate the superiority of their new-fangled religions and
their pagan ethics to what they tried so hard to dismiss as the
old-fashioned faith and ethics of historic religion. And they
made the most of chance—give them credit! They tried to
build a civilization on power and wealth and special privilege
for special races and special nations and special peoples. The
blasted face of Europe, the burning face of Asia, and the heart
of fear throughout the world today are eloquent testimonials to
the thoroughness of their efforts.

Small wonder, then, that men like Mr. Priestley are ready to
admit their error and openly to express a longing for a "place
of worship"! But where to look? Some new religion, new cult,
new sect, or the Church? Is the Church, is *this* Church, the place
of worship they seek? This probing question cannot be answered
in one effort—but we can at least make a beginning with the
fundamental question that the seekers of this generation are
sure to raise: *What Is the Church?* In answer to this query, I
should like to make two simple declarative statements of fact
about the Church. One is more or less objective in nature and
the other more or less subjective, but both are important to an
understanding of the Church.

II

The first fact is as objective as sunshine and obvious to anyone who has a reading knowledge of history. Even if we cannot
get some of our critics to enter a church building, they can
appreciate this fact! *The Church is the institution dedicated to
the perpetuation of a religious tradition.* The Christian Church

is dedicated to the perpetuation of the Christian tradition. Vital religion always expresses itself in and through some kind of institution. But for the institution, the insights of faith would have perished rather than have been perpetuated in a tradition and thereby made available to subsequent generations. There doubtless have been many noble insights here, there and yonder in the human scene over these tens of thousands of years that have blazed up like candles in the dark only to go out because they were not perpetuated by some institution. No one knows how much squandering of spiritual capital there has been in the long range of human history because of this oft-repeated and always tragic fact. This is a good time—and a very good company in which—to acknowledge our debt of gratitude to the schools of disciples who gathered around men like Jeremiah, Isaiah and Amos. But for them we might not now know so much as the names of these spiritual giants. But thanks to these "schools" of earnest followers, we know their names and much of what they thought and said in their day and generation. We are not so fortunate as regards many other prophetic figures. They were hermits, living alone, separating themselves from any kind of institution or social group through which their insights might be passed on to subsequent generations. We scarcely know their names.

The Christian faith has expressed itself through not only one but many different forms of social organization. I do believe we have tried every conceivable kind of social organization within the Christian Church over the nineteen hundred years of Christian history. We have churches with and without stated liturgies, with and without bishops, with and without preachers, with and without sacraments, with and without centralized institutional government. Some critics would dismiss the Church as being hopelessly divided because of such broad differences. Yet they overlook the unity in purpose which binds all branches of the Christian Church into a Church. And Dean Willard Sperry has put that purpose in these words: "It is the business of the Church to make God real to every generation." There's a purpose for you—one guaranteed to kindle our imagination and loyalty as nothing else could!

It is a matter of historical record and achievement that the Church has accomplished this purpose with some measure of real success. Its growth and spread constitute one of the most amazing facts in human history. Beginning with a handful of persons living in a relatively small area of the eastern part of the Graeco-Roman world, it has spread to the corners of the earth in less than two thousand years. It has crossed all known borders and barriers that usually separate men: clan, race, nation, culture. Though it has taken on (and cast off) many different social forms, the purpose of and in each was the ancient goal of the disciples: to preach Christ to all men. The true marvel of the Church is the tremendous loyalty of its different forms to the single purpose of the Christian faith.

When various forms of the Church today trumpet abroad the claim that they are "the only true form," it is well to listen quietly, even respectfully, without forgetting the multiple forms through which the Christian faith has asserted itself in the lives of men. Whether, in our creeds, we say we believe in the "one catholic and apostolic Church," or in the "holy catholic Church," or in "the Church as the fellowship for worship and for service of all who are united to the Living Lord," we are pointing a steady finger at the fact that the Church has been and is the actual interpreter of the Christian faith through the ages.

III

You who ask "What Is the Church?" must now enter the church building to appreciate the richness and importance of the second fact that goes into the answer to your question. *The Church is a religious fellowship; a fellowship of people engaged in doing many different things but, again, with one basic purpose in view.* Let me be your guide, as it were, as we move through the Church in our attempt to get at the fact underlying the second claim. Wanting to put first things first, to begin at the beginning, in order that you may understand the deep unifying purpose of all that goes on here, I ask you to note the people engaged in worship. Not only in this service and in this room, but wherever we meet as churchmen, we bow in reverence before the Most High God. What we do, as churchmen, we do or try to do *"Under God,"* that is, with an alert, humble awareness of Him and His will. Oh, I know, this act of devotion can be as perfunctory in the Church as it was in a certain businessmen's group where I was asked to give the invocation. The "Amen" had not ceased echoing in the room before the chairman said, "Now, let's get down to business." I could not resist asking, "What do you think we've been doing?" If our acts of worship are casual, forced, perfunctory, here, then, to that extent, we miss the deepest and truest fact about our fellowship.

For the *Church is a sanctuary;* it is the place and the people who consciously and deliberately cultivate the practice of the worship of God. This is the true foundation of the Church's purpose, the true meaning of her life. She is not an end in herself, she is the means to the end of the Will of God. She is not God! She is a finger pointing at the fact of God. Formal worship services are little more than solemn and, I'm afraid, rather dull spectacles if they do not somehow enable the participant to glimpse anew the glory of God which is trying to burst through the hymns, scripture, prayer and sermon. The first and fundamental movement in the life of the Church is this mood of worship—a sincere worship of the living God.

And the God we seek in worship is and must be a living God. He is not simply Someone who was real to Moses and Isaiah: he must be Someone who is trying to be as real to us and to all men as He was to them. It is this vivid sense of the presence of the Living God that gives a worship service its soul, its reason for being. Without this awareness of God, it is little more than a parade of archaic forms; with it, worship can be lips cleansed and consecrated by divine fire, a life recalled from aimlessness and redeemed in Divine Purpose.

The forms we use in services of worship are important but decidedly secondary to the aim of worship. Insistence upon some particular liturgical form as the only proper one is a familiar form of idol worship in churches. There is no one final form for the worship of the Living God. Elijah heard the voice of God in the stillness which followed the storms of fire and wind; Isaiah heard it beating through the moving ritual of the Temple; John Woolman heard it in the period of quiet of the early Quaker societies; John Wesley heard it in the shouted hymns of Welsh coal miners. But whatever the differences in the circumstances of its coming, it produced a single effect upon them; it galvanized them into action in the name and in the service of God. Worship is man earnestly endeavoring to confront God; it is man humbly but courageously trying to think God's thoughts after Him; it is man trying to get some clear insight into God's will for his life. As such, worship humbles the pride and indicts the self-righteousness of men—for in the sight of God "all have sinned and come short of the glory of God." Having stripped man of the tinsel trappings of feigned virtue and false pride, worship reveals the true glory of a life dedicated to, lost in, the will of God.

Study the Church at worship and you discover that the deepest fact about her is the consciousness of belonging, not to this preacher or to this congregation or to this age, *but to God.*

This fact never had more dramatic utterance than in the stumbling words of a native chieftain, on an island in the South Seas, by the name of Jason. He and his tribe—all Christians—had built a chapel commemorating the sixteen hundred American men who fell in battle there. As Jason presented the chapel to the American chaplain, he said, "We want tell you all people that we fella belong Solomon build this church because we want thank you. Now we give this church you. But this church no belong you and me. This church belong God!"

So I say to you, my critical guest, *The Church is a Sanctuary.*

IV

But the Church is something more; *she is a school for young and old alike.* How could it be otherwise? We do not start from scratch with our own experiences in religion. We would be incredibly poor if that were true. We stand before the cornucopia of three thousand years of human experience and seek to weigh our inheritance. The Bible itself is a rich record of nearly half of that period of time, and Church history and tradition pour the rest at our feet. Therefore we teach the Bible in our school here, and we seek to make it live not only in terms of the day in which it was written but in terms of our own as well. So also with our Church traditions. Our church school is dedicated to the task of helping us become alert, literate, convinced citizens of the entire religious heritage of mankind, with especial emphasis upon the Hebrew-Christian tradition.

I wish I could be sure we adults agreed among ourselves on the urgency of this task of religious education! The Church must pursue her mission in an increasingly literate world. "Educate or perish" is the law of survival for social institutions today as never before. Education is big business in this country. It involves the expenditure of billions of dollars, the life energies of many industries. Laws require children to go to school for a longer period of their life than ever before. With all the sentiment for lower taxes, no seasoned political leader would think of decreasing the amount of public monies which flow into the school systems. It is much safer to present himself as one who wants *better schools*. I have lived through the heat of many municipal elections without seeing one exception to this rule. The rule holds because people want a good educational system. They may be confused about what constitutes "good"; they may want it without being willing to pay for it—but the all-important point for us just now is *that they want it*.

The newspaper, radio, motion picture and television are powerful media for driving home ideas, suggesting attitudes, cultivating tastes, formulating opinion on matters of morals, manners and practices. Indeed, they are so powerful that they come to us bearing a blessing or a curse, depending upon the use to which they are put. Whatever the Church teaches must be presented in terms as vital, as relevant, as sensible as anything our students hear elsewhere.

So we say to those who ask "What Is the Church?", the Church is a school, and is trying to be a good school.

V

In addition to being a sanctuary and a *school,* the Church is a "nucleus of brotherhood." Historically, the Church began in the homes of the faithful. Too few to need and too poor to build a separate building for worship, they gathered in the largest of their homes at the close of day for an evening meal and a service of worship. The letters of Paul are eloquent with incidents that must have given the early groups lively concern.

The problem of any one of the brotherhood was the problem of all. Paul makes it clear that there was something downright disgraceful in two Christians pressing a quarrel between themselves to the point that they were haled before a heathen judge for trial! He discusses any and all of the problems that agitated the lives of his flock. His lash always fell on those practices and attitudes which tended to separate or destroy the unity of the Church. To him as to every great Christian spirit in subsequent generations, unity and community are to be the tokens of Christian fellowship. "By this shall all men know that ye are my disciples, that ye love one another."

The ministry of brotherhood is an indispensable part of the work of the Church. For man is a social being. He was not meant to live alone, but in communion with others. When, for any reason, the bonds that bind a man to a given group are severed, instead of being freed thereby, he is more frequently lost. This point was driven home for me some years ago when a man sought me out at the conclusion of a Christmas carol service in our church in Baltimore. He said, "I would give $25,000 for a Christmas card." As his story unfolded, I learned that his home was broken, largely through his own fault, and he was separated from his wife and two grown children for the first time at Christmas. The freedom he had sought and found was bringing him little joy—so little that he longed for some symbol of continuing concern and care on their part. When none was forthcoming, his life literally trembled on the brink of suicide. At my suggestion, he agreed to try to build a new life, beginning within the Church. Through four long years—before his business took him elsewhere—he was a faithful and creative member of that church. For four years the ministry of fellowship (extended all unaware of his special need) of that congregation enfolded him, drained the poisons off his wounds, healed him, and set him on his feet and way again. As he took leave of us, he said, "I have found my way again!"

The Church, to be true to her vision, must extend the mantle of brotherhood to all men evenly. A class Church, or a race Church, or a national Church are contradictions in terms, since they attempt to include some and exclude others of the human family from the fellowship of the Church. In so far as the Church permits herself to become identified with some part or fragment or segment of mankind, she ceases to speak a universal message. The rapid growth of the ecumenical Church in our time is evidence of the desire of churches to center attention upon their points of unity rather than of disunity. Every ounce of influence and encouragement we can exert in this effort is all to the good for, basically, the Church is a *fellowship* as well as a *sanctuary* and a *school:* a fellowship in which men and people *"find their way again."*

VI

One further fact about the Church is this: *She is a Crusade!* How some shrink back from the clear implications of that! For some the aversion may be so pronounced as to be visceral in character! Yet the Church must have a ministry of social conscience if she would be true to her Lord, her Gospel and her history. Lest timid Methodists think this is a concoction of fellow travelers and radicals hear these memorable words of the Encyclical Letter which conveyed the results of the Lambeth Conference of 1948 to the Protestant Episcopal Church of the World:

The Church is the champion of men against all that cheapens and degrades him: for the gospel is the charter of man's dignity. The mission of the Church, now as always, is to proclaim and live out the Gospel by which alone men can be saved from sin and judgment, and the world from despair and self-destruction. . . . We must bring the teaching and example of Christ into our everyday lives. . . . Nothing that is good in the sight of God should be outside the Church's interest.

When Episcopalians talk that way, Methodists surely have plenty of elbow room for social action! Theoretically, the Church has seldom taken any other position than this, but, actually, she has been most reluctant to take this one seriously. Now, with the sands of time about run out of the hourglass of our civilization, she is getting down to business, so to speak.

The Church has no choice but to accept as her own any and every sincere concern and problem of her people. To do less is to admit her irrelevance at precisely those points where she has or ought to have the most to contribute. That the acceptance of this strategy will bring every controversial issue of the day before the Church for consideration and judgment goes without saying. This need not and should not transform the Church into either a forum on public affairs or a debating society. But it does clearly mean that the Church will create ways and means of giving controversial issues a most careful and conscientious hearing. Some churches have social action committees that are charged with the responsibility of keeping the Church informed on all such issues. In others, the minister in his preaching strives to interpret the implications of the faith for the issues at hand. The ecumenical conferences of 1937 and 1948 spent considerable time seeking and clarifying the Church's responsibility on social issues. This much is clear: every church worthy of the name will be a crusading fellowship.

This, then, is the Church: She is an institution dedicated to the perpetuation of a religious tradition; she is a fellowship in worship, study, brotherhood and redemptive action. Yet this is more, much more, than a precious heritage. It is a trust, a sacred trust, given us by our fathers before us. It is our high calling to stand in this tradition; to receive, to share and to pass it on to our children strengthened and enriched by the life and work of our generation. Hard work? Of course it is! Rewarding work? The most rewarding in the world! With a full consciousness of this, of what it means in work over the years ahead, I salute you who are this Church with the words with which an early Christian pastor welcomed converts into the Church: "You are a chosen race, a royal priesthood, a holy nation, God's own people, that you may declare the wonderful deeds of him who called you out of darkness into his marvelous light."

8 What the Church Owes You

And he spake a parable unto them, Can the blind lead the blind? shall they not both fall into the ditch?

The disciple is not above his master: but every one that is perfect shall be as his master.

And why beholdest thou the mote that is in thy brother's eye, but perceivest not the beam that is in thine own eye?

Either how canst thou say to thy brother, Brother, let me pull out the mote that is in thine eye, when thou thyself beholdest not the beam that is in thine own eye? Thou hypocrite, cast out first the beam out of thine own eye, and then shalt thou see clearly to pull out the mote that is in thy brother's eye.

For a good tree bringeth not forth corrupt fruit; neither doth a corrupt tree bring forth good fruit.

For every tree is known by his own fruit. For of thorns men do not gather figs, nor of a bramble bush gather they grapes.

A good man out of the good treasure of his heart bringeth forth that which is good; and an evil man out of the evil treasure of his heart bringeth forth that which is evil; for of the abundance of the heart his mouth speaketh.

St. Luke 6:39–45

I

THE urgency of an exploration of the relationship between individuals and churches is found in the simple
statistical fact that less than half of the adults in this avowedly
Christian country belong to any Church, Protestant or Catholic,
and a considerable number of those who do belong to one or
the other fall into that highly dubious and very populous
category—"nominal members."

On the face of it, then, the majority of our contemporaries
are, to put it mildly, not enough impressed with the Church to
participate actively in her life and purpose. Yet, many of these
selfsame people expect the Church to live and grow and be a
power for good in our common life. They are typified by a
friend of mine who was a nominal member of our Church in
the East. We happened to meet one day shortly after Pearl
Harbor. He said, "You fellows had better get busy or this world
is going to the devil for sure." I asked, "What do you mean,
'You fellows'? It's as much your job as mine to try to get things
headed in the right direction." It is difficult to stifle the impulse
to chide such people, but that would be too easy and almost
certainly would be unfair both to them and to the Church.
It is, however, both proper and necessary to point out to non-
Christians and nominal Christians that they cannot have it both
ways; that they must make up their minds whether they want
a powerful Church, a weak Church, or no Church at all. But
having done that, an immensely more useful task remains to be
tackled, namely, to clarify the relationship between man and
the Church, between people like us and a Church like this.

Some years ago, I was confronting a student conference with
the claim that they ought to ally themselves with the Church
and work in and through it. In the question period, a young
man put this typically forthright question, "Why should I join

the Church? What's in it for me?" I like that question. It need be neither selfish nor impertinent. If asked honestly, it is one way to the heart of the matter before us, and deserves an honest answer. It certainly clears the all too murky atmosphere which so easily and frequently shrouds the Church. Every member of the Church ought to welcome it and be able to answer it in an intelligent and persuasive fashion. And every person outside the Church is entitled to stay outside—and with a clear conscience!—until he gets a convincing answer.

Let us practice what we preach and put first things first in this study of what the Church owes you. One obligation above all others the Church owes every human being, every institution, and every social order known to man—the proclamation of the gospel: The proclamation of the fact that Jesus Christ is our clearest revelation of the will of God for the life of man; that in his life and teachings we have a lucid insight into, and a powerful exemplification of, the love of God; that in his will are both our judgment and our peace. This gospel is the Church's peculiar heritage, and the proclamation of it her most pressing duty. This fact has been held high by every ecumenical conference in recent years, and we may be sure it will be exalted again when the World Council of Churches holds its first American meeting in Evanston in 1954. The Church is an institution with a divine duty, a fellowship pregnant with divine purpose, a group of people like us willing to hear and determined to heed and proclaim as best we can the will of God as we see it in Jesus Christ. We do not have a variety of gospels: One for the educated and another for the uneducated; one for the sophisticated and another for the naïve; one for the rich and another for the poor; one for the powerful and another for the weak; one for the saints and another for the sinners; one for the communist and another for the capitalist. We have one gospel—and the Church owes you, no matter who you are, the confrontation of your total life by that gospel.

But once we accept this duty as the overarching obligation of the Church, our task, while well under way, is far from finished. We must get down to cases, as practical men like to say. You who belong to other religions—what does the Church owe you? You who are outside the Church—what does the Church owe you? You who are inside the Church—what does the Church owe you? And is it possible for us to summarize the Church's obligation to this confused, fearful, bellicose world of ours?

II

The problem of what the Christian Church owes non-Christian groups may seem far-fetched to a Church and community like this but it is one of the most far-flung problems faced by the Church today. One great missionary conference after another has wrestled with it, and book after book has been written about it—one of the best by a member of our own church, Edmund D. Soper, now in India. We begin with the realization that there are many, many more non-Christians than Christians in the world today. Rough estimates reveal the fact that among the people on the face of this earth there are 246,000,000 Mohammedans, 240,000,000 Hindus, 137,000,000 Buddhists, 17,000,000 Jews and just about 1,000,000,000 pagans of one sort or another. There is no point pretending that the Christian faith has the world to itself even though it claims 600,000,000 adherents in all groups. We cannot say with Falstaff:

> Why, then the world's mine oyster
> Which I with sword will open.

We owe other religions the simple awareness that we share responsibility for the spiritual concerns of mankind with them; that we honor them for what they are and do; that we seek a good working knowledge of them; that there ought to be a serious and sustained effort to find common ground for thought and action with them. That this can and ought to be done without losing or watering down the gospel has been the stated conviction of every great missionary conference for the last forty years. Seeking, as we say we are, to build a firm spiritual foundation for this tottering old world, we shall need to work with all forces seeking that same end.

III

Turn now to the problem faced by the Church as she confronts half of the adults in these United States—What does the Church owe you who are outside the Church? She owes you four things, most of which are too obvious to need more than mention, yet, when taken together, mean or ought to mean much to you.

First, she owes you friendly encouragement to investigate the Church in every phase of her life. The Church invites you to ask any question that occurs to you as you seek better to know what the Church is and tries to be. You will not find the sign "No criticism please" anywhere in the life of a Church that is earnestly trying to do her job. You have the right, yes, the obligation, to ask questions and keep right on asking them until you get a satisfactory answer. You may find that your quest will take you from one branch of the Church to another. If so, well and good if the end result is a vital creative relationship between you and the Church.

Second, the Church owes you an honest answer to your questions. You have a right to be on your guard at once when a

Church asks that you be prepared to take on faith anything she chooses to affirm and then trots out a succession of irrational and fundamentally ridiculous doctrines, dogmas and practices that you are supposed to embrace. There are churches, both Protestant and Catholic, that do just that, I am sorry to say. You will be the poorer if you accept their ultimatum and permit the anesthetizing of your intelligence as a necessary first step to fellowship in the Church. Let there be no misunderstanding on this point: Honest answers can be given to honest questions, and serious questions should be insisted upon until such an answer is forthcoming.

Third, the Church owes you a decent respect for your reason, judgment and decision. If you choose not to investigate the Church, or, having done it to your satisfaction, choose to stay outside the Church, the Church ought to honor your decision and not lapse into carping criticism, if not outright persecution. Persecution, whether in aggravated or mild form, of unbelievers and skeptics is out—and out forever so far as an increasing number of Protestant churches are concerned. We renounce root and branch the Roman Catholic doctrine that "error does not have the same rights as truth"—the doctrine that was the basis of the Inquisition and that offers the permanent threat of persecution of non-Roman Catholics wherever the Church is able to become the State Church. Francis Cardinal Spellman would call me "a bigot" for making that statement, I know. I know, too, that that is his standard answer to any criticism of his Church. This assertion so far from being an expression of prejudice on my part can be documented in detail by actual events in a dozen countries over the last five years.

We renounce that doctrine for two very good reasons. To begin with, we are acquainted with our debt to many who were denounced as blasphemers and heretics in earlier generations. Jesus, Paul, Galileo, Bruno, Luther, Calvin, Wesley—all were denounced because they had chosen to break with traditional patterns of thought and life. But they were right in every major way, and history—even the history of the institutions that cast them out—bears witness to that dissent. This, actually, is the second reason why we renounce the doctrinal basis of persecution—we have so much yet to learn before we know the perfect will of God that we are ready to listen to all who think they can help. That does not mean that we have lost confidence in our Church or religious convictions—far from that! It means, rather, we have enough confidence in them that we need not disguise their shortcomings or inadequacies by an effort to silence the ones who might be able to help us.

If you choose to stay outside the Church, she should not give you the impression that she is washing her hands of you! Her respect for your decision should take the affirmative form of being willing to work with you for humane ends even though we travel parallel paths of motive toward those ends. Further, she ought always to be ready to share your problems and needs whenever you will permit. The God whom we seek to serve is no less concerned about you and your welfare because you are outside the Church, and neither are we.

One last thing the Church owes you who are outside: An untiring effort to win your understanding, your loyalty, your fellowship in the Church. We shall hope not to harass you with our efforts or bother you with our good intentions, but we cannot give up trying. The Church needs you—this we know; and you need the Church—this we believe. Before you are through with the Church or the Church is through with you, we may feel like a certain young woman who after four years of being besieged by insistent, unrelenting, impetuous, importunate courtship married the man, explaining with a twinkle in her eyes, "That was the only way I could get rid of him!"

IV

Having served this friendly notice of our intentions toward you who are outside the Church, we come to the question of what the Church owes you who are in the Church.

The most important thing she owes you—and most important because it is fundamental to everything she may try to do—is a warm, creative, religious fellowship. Those interlocking adjectives—*warm, creative, religious*—are important because they describe the genius of a Church that is really a fellowship. *Warm:* You ought to feel at home here, feel that you belong, feel needed and wanted and welcome. *Creative:* This fellowship should encourage you to find and use your talents; it should offer you opportunity to know people who will stimulate you, help you build new confidence in yourself and other people; it should confront you with opportunities for helping others less fortunate than yourself. *Religious:* We seek to be God's people, a people who consciously try to center their thought and life in God. We fail often enough—no one knows that better than we do—but we do know it and turn away from each betrayal determined to do better. The distinctions that seem to matter so much to so many—race, class, position, wealth, education—simply do not rate as being ultimately important in this religious fellowship. And when we, through our humanity, let them sway our judgment and attention, then we, through our Christian conscience, are brought low in penitence and humility before the God whose love for all is unqualifiedly equal.

Within the context of this sort of fellowship, the Church owes you a careful statement of faith and continuous instruction therein. That has been and will remain one of the primary obligations of the preaching industry of the Church. And it is the reason why we have, and must have, a Church School. It is an ideal, we know, but we propose to continue to hope and work toward the day when every member of the Church will be able to give a reason—and a good reason—for the hope that is within him; when every child who goes through our Church School will know what we believe, why we believe it, what we propose to do about it, and will feel personally persuaded to share it. That this means more—much more—careful attention on the part of all of us, not just a few of us, to the total educational program of the entire Church—in the Church School, the Woman's Society of Christian Service, the Men's Club, the Methodist Youth Fellowship, as well as in every other group, goes without saying. The greatest truths on earth deserve the greatest teachers on earth and the most efficient educational program we can devise, and the heartfelt co-operation of everyone.

In addition, the Church owes its members a realistic consideration of the main issues of our time in the light of the Christian ethic. Nothing human is alien to our concern; the world continues to be our parish; we must continue to confront men in need with the good news that there is a way through and beyond their troubles. The pulpit, the classroom, the Church groups, and the Church press must link hands in the tremendous task of bringing the problems of the whole world before the judgment bar of the will of God as seen in Jesus Christ. This is not to say that we have all the answers and, given the chance, will solve all problems, but it is to say that until and unless men are willing to look at their problems in this light, they never will find the right answers. And it must be expected that the answers suggested by the Christian faith will frequently be revolutionary in the extreme. How could it be otherwise? Can anyone think that the kingdoms of this world will be made over into the Kingdom of our Lord without radical transformation? We do no one a service, and we do the Christian faith a distinct disservice, when we seek to soft-pedal this fact.

You who are members of the Church have a right to expect that the Church will help you understand what you are up against in the battle of life, that she will furnish you the moral support of a vital fellowship as you try to translate your faith into life. She owes you the irreplaceable strength that comes through the worship of the living God and fellowship with others both in worship and in service. For you, this means strength for today, hope for tomorrow, and courage for both.

V

And what does the Church owe the world? Many things to be sure, but these most of all:

First, a steady witness to the fact of God as seen in Jesus Christ. The God in whom we believe is the Judge of all the earth, the One "who rebuketh strong nations from afar," whose mighty will is the moral order of the world. There is nothing weak about Him who holds all in the hollow of His hand. In the stirring words of Isaiah, the God of the universe is One before whom "the nations are as a drop of a bucket, and are counted as the small dust of the balance. . . ." There's an adequate antidote for our pride in the power of armies, navies and all the panoply of modern nations! Nations are like the dust on scales which the careful merchant blows off as he goes about his business! Which is great religion's way of saying that God is the ultimate Fact and Factor in this universe, and we either find Him or perish. As old as, yes, much older than, Isaiah, the proclamation of this message continues to be one of the obligations of the Church today. Not that it is always a welcome task!

It is both a salutary and a difficult thing for proud and

powerful peoples to be confronted at the height of their power
by the fact of God and his judgment upon them. When Rudyard Kipling was asked to write an ode for Queen Victoria's
Jubilee which had been a parade of the power of Britain, he
wrote "Recessional." Many a Britain thought it in poor taste
and quite unworthy of that great occasion. Rumor has it that
Her Majesty and her councils were highly incensed with these
lines:

> For heathen heart that puts her trust
>   In reeking tube and iron shard—
> All valiant dust that builds on dust,
>   And guarding, calls not Thee to guard—
> For frantic boast and foolish word,
>   Thy mercy on Thy people, Lord! [1]

If you think this presumptuous of Kipling, then the Psalmist
too was presumptuous when he wrote: "Except the Lord build
a house they labor in vain that built it; except the Lord keep
the city the watchmen waketh but in vain." It is one of the
permanent obligations of the Christian Church to engage in
that kind of presumption. There is no other way to keep men
and nations from the pitfall of pride. The effort to strike the
blinders of pride from our eyes, to keep people humble before
God, humble enough to cry, "God be merciful to me a sinner"
instead of, "Lord, I thank thee that I am not as other men"—
this is one of the Church's most important tasks as we seek to
ward off the catastrophe which now threatens us all.

A second obligation the Church owes the world is an example of the fellowship that actually heals the wounds and
bridges the chasms that separate us from one another. We are

[1] From *The Five Nations* by Rudyard Kipling, copyright, 1903, 1931,
by Rudyard Kipling. Reprinted by permission of Doubleday & Company, Mrs. George Bambridge, and the Macmillan Company of Canada,
Ltd.

called upon to lift our common life to the highest possible levels of brotherhood, compassion and love. Instead of finding in the Church an extension and tacit extenuation of our prejudices and divisions, the world ought to be rebuked at the point of her divisions by the demonstration of unity and fellowship in the Church. The Church's most effective critique of the sins of the world will never be what she says; it will be what she is and does. And the Church that does not criticize the world for conscience' sake will soon find that she has lost both her conscience and desire to criticize anyone for anything.

The Church owes the world a steady demonstration of the kind of spiritual unity that is deeper and stronger than loyalty to nation, or race, or class, or creed. And the Church that shrinks back from that exacting duty would do well to hear again an ancient indictment of her:

> Say to the Church it shows
> What's good, and doth no good.

Thank God, Churches are not wholly remiss in this great matter. We are learning how to work together; we have come a long way already but a longer road stretches ahead of us. We shall be doing nothing more important as a Church than giving every encouragement and support to this journey toward real unity. This is an obligation to the world we will not want to neglect.

As I have been running swiftly over these obligations of the Church to people of other religions, to people outside and inside the Church, and to the world in general, you must have been asking with Paul, "Who is sufficient for these things?" And, I confess, I share that question. Each time I find myself wondering about the meaning and value of the Church and what we do in the name of the Church, my answer comes not from the tomes of theology but from testimonies like these three.

Present at every Sunday morning service of the church I attended as a boy was a woman who drove in from a farm several miles away. Illness might keep her away but never company or fatigue or the weather—good or bad. When asked why she came so faithfully she replied simply, "Sometimes it helps."

I have worked my way, page by page, through the records of the great conferences of churches as they discussed the nature and work of the Church and, I give you my word, none of them ever put a finger more squarely on what the Church means to people like us than did one of the laymen in the second church I served. It was in a rural village during the depression that hit the Midwest farm area in the 1920's. I remember my discouragement when some of the faint-hearted wondered whether they should even try to keep the church open any longer. If I live to be a hundred, I shall never forget the answer one of the older men gave to the doubters, "We need a place to worship the Almighty, to baptize our babies, to teach our children, to marry our young people, and to bury our dead." There you have it—the Church at work in the life of man!

And lest we think this is purely an "insider's" view of the value of the work of the Church, hear what a conscientious young Brahmin told Dr. Arthur Holt when the latter was in India a few years ago. "I want to go back to serve the villages, and I wish that we Hindus had a church back there which would give me my support and let me serve unselfishly the cause of village reconstruction. But the temple where I used to worship, although it is endowed, is falling into ruins, and the endowment has been appropriated by a few selfish people and used for their own advantage. I wish there was a church which would give me backing the way your Christian churches give backing to your young men who go even to foreign lands to serve the good cause."

Let testimonies like these then be food for our spirit as we

engage in the work of the Church today, and let the words of
the hymn be the prayer of our common life in this Church:

> O Spirit of the Living God,
>   Thou Light and Fire Divine:
> Descend upon Thy Church once more
>   And make it truly Thine!
>
> Teach us to utter living words
>   Of truth which all may hear,
> The language all men understand
>   When love speaks, loud and clear.
>
> Till every age and race and clime
>   Shall blend their creeds in one,
> And earth shall form one brotherhood
>   By whom Thy will is done!

9 What You Owe the Church

SCRIPTURE LESSON

For, brethren, ye have been called unto liberty; only use not liberty for an occasion to the flesh, but by love serve one another.

For all the law is fulfilled in one word, even in this; Thou shalt love thy neighbour as thyself.

But if ye bite and devour one another, take heed that ye be not consumed one of another.

This I say then, Walk in the Spirit, and ye shall not fulfill the lust of the flesh.

For the flesh lusteth against the Spirit, and the Spirit against the flesh: and these are contrary the one to the other: so that ye cannot do the things that ye would.

But if ye be led of the Spirit, ye are not under the law.

Now the works of the flesh are manifest, which are these: Adultery, fornication, uncleanness, lasciviousness,

Idolatry, witchcraft, hatred, variance, emulations, wrath, strife, seditions, heresies,

Envyings, murders, drunkenness, revellings, and such like: of the which I tell you before, as I have also told you in time past, that they which do such things shall not inherit the kingdom of God.

But the fruit of the Spirit is love, joy, peace, longsuffering, gentleness, goodness, faith,

Meekness, temperance: against such there is no law.

And they that are Christ's have crucified the flesh with the affections and lusts.

If we live in the Spirit, let us also walk in the Spirit.

GALATIANS 5:13–25

I

THE question of what you owe the Church can best be answered by summarizing an obligation and suggesting an opportunity.

And that obligation—that awareness of what we owe the Church, of the enormous contributions which the Church has made and continues to make to us and to our common life—is clear cut and beyond the reach of a reasonable dispute. I am not blind to the fact that it is still possible to hear gifted amateurs toss off judgments on the Church that are supposed to dismiss her from the sacred precincts of intellectual respectability. That same sort of thing has been going on for nearly two thousand years now. It must be downright discouraging to the proud authors of such judgments to see how the Church, like Ol' Man River, "jest keeps rollin' along." I emphasize the fact that, as a rule, amateurs are the authors of such judgments. Serious students of the human scene know better, and are prompt and unequivocal in their acknowledgment of obligation to the Church in many fundamental matters.

In this day when the writings of Arnold Toynbee have been widely read and even more widely quoted, most of us have encountered his famous description of the Christian Church as the "carrier of culture" from the classical civilizations of the Mediterranean to the new civilizations centered in Northern Europe and Western Asia. That phrase "carrier of culture" is packed with meaning—enough meaning, in fact, to command respect for the Church from anyone—whether inside or outside the Church. Translate it into ideas, ideals and institutions, and its meaning becomes most compelling. The Christian Church was the custodian of several great ideas which set in motion some of the most important influences in Western culture. She received the idea of *Faith* from Judaism, *Knowledge and Beauty* from Greece, *Law and Order* from Rome, and *Love and Brotherhood* from the early Christian community. These ideas were not abstractions when she got them. They were incarnate in systems of thought, codes of law, works of art, sacred writings and actual communities of people. When the schools, governments, temples and other institutions of the ancient civilizations collapsed, the Christian Church found herself in the possession of these tremendous deposits of human experience and insight. For a long time the Church, like many another heir, was not aware of the priceless character of her inheritance. Some of it she neglected, some she distorted, some she denied, some she used wisely and well, but—and this is Toynbee's point and the one I want to underscore just now—she brought it all along with her as she journeyed through the years. With every passing century more and more men became aware of this heritage and began to study it and apply it to the problems they faced.

The result? Schools, libraries, hospitals, humane institutions of every kind came into existence. Systems of thought, probing ethical ideals, movement after movement aiming at social reform grew to maturity—not in a night, to be sure, but over generations of men with awakening minds, spirits and consciences. Philosophers, theologians, artists, reformers, teachers, doctors and scientists—all found stimulation, insight and encouragement from this heritage—even when they may have had trouble with the Church herself on other scores. Wittingly or unwittingly, willingly or unwillingly, consciously or unconsciously, the Church was the carrier of some of the most creative and powerful cultural ideas and influences ever to be let loose in human history. In calling attention to this fact, I am but summarizing an obligation that every living man owes the Church whether he is inside or outside the Church.

If you think I have overstated the case, try this experiment.

Imagine, if you can, Western civilization stripped not only of
the Church herself but of the cultural heritage she brought to
it and the impulses and institutions which have radiated out
from her. The skyline of every town in Europe and America
would be altered as if by a direct bomb hit because the churches
and cathedrals would disappear. What a change that would
make! One evening not long ago I saw some beautiful pictures
of European towns, taken by one of our families the previous
summer. Every hamlet or city was dominated by the spire or
dome of some church. Oh, to be sure, with the churches gone,
you would have something left of the villages. You would have
great libraries and art galleries left in large cities. But wait!
We must go through these libraries and take out every book
that exhibits any indebtedness to the Church. We must go
through the Louvre and do the same. The major creations of
Michelangelo, Raphael, Leonardo and others will have to go.
Much would be left, I know, but I wonder whether anyone
could contemplate it without being made all the more conscious
of the grandeur that was gone.

Without carrying this experiment in imagination any further, we may safely predict that if ever we should try to subtract
the Church and all she has both brought to, and meant in,
Western culture from that culture, and if we should achieve
some success at it, much of our cultural heritage would remain—like a body remains in death after the warmth, radiance
and power of the spirit have fled.

Walter Lippmann, who, I think, cannot be accused of being
swayed by a possible professional bias in such matters, put his
finger squarely on one of our greatest obligations to the Church
in a column he wrote during the dark days of World War II.
As I recall, he was trying to get to the heart of the matter as
to what constitutes the binding element in Western civilization.
He says that it is the moral and spiritual heritage of the Hebrew-

Christian tradition. This is the seedbed of the great ideas of democracy, freedom and justice. Wherever this religious tradition has gone, these ideas have sprung up.

Take a quick look at the facts, and you will see how right Mr. Lippmann is in this thesis. The Christian conception that man is the bearer of intrinsic worth because he is the child of God is fundamental to what we mean by "the good society." The Christian conception of freedom—freedom before man and God, a freedom which must finally spell itself out in terms of responsible living with man and God—this conception underlies the ideal of freedom which has played so large a role in the thought and life of the Western world.

I am not claiming—in fact I should be the first to disclaim— that the Christian Church has been the good preacher and practitioner of these great conceptions that she should have been. But I do say—and with complete confidence—that without her life and ministry these ideas would not have become the powers they have been and are in our common life. And it is a reasonable conclusion that anyone who treasures democracy, freedom and the good society as ideals for us and our children will be willing to acknowledge his indebtedness to the Christian Church. It is no accident that the Church is one of the first institutions to go under the fire of any person or power bent on subverting or destroying these ideals and the institutions they helped create. That, I am sure, is sound strategy. So long as the Church stands and preaches the gospel, no power on earth can hope either to destroy or to keep down forever these great banners under which men have sought to march toward the abundant life.

Whether we are inside or outside the Church, we benefit by her life and labors over twenty preceding centuries. This is the most important general fact to keep in mind as we proceed

with a closer scrutiny of what "outsiders" and "insiders" owe
the Church.

II

What do you who are outside the Church owe her? Several
obligations stand out.

1. Elemental fairness requires that you neither try to deny or
belittle her contributions, past and present, to you personally
and to our way of life. She has been a formative fact in the
development of our culture; she is a powerful fact in our
common life. Although her power has frequently served the
ends of intolerance and persecution—as in Catholic Spain and
Puritan New England—the sum total of her influence has been
for the ennoblement and strengthening of human life. It is the
mark of immaturity to let the exceptions cancel out the rule—as
so many people do who disclaim the Church in her entirety
because of what she has done upon occasion. You who are
outside the Church owe her an honest accounting in such matters—and, I may say, she welcomes such an accounting.

2. You owe her a serious and sustained effort to understand
her conception of herself and her work. She is like no other
institution known to man. She claims to be in the world but
not of the world. She claims to be a creature of eternity living
in time. She insists that she seeks a city not made with hands,
yet works steadily at the creation of the city of God in the life
of man. She is composed of people like us yet claims she is the
Body of our Living Lord. She knows that her people are
citizens of various social orders yet insist that she gather them
into a fellowship that transcends our social orders and makes
them citizens of the Kingdom of God. Though swayed by the
ways of the society in which she lives and works, she denies
that she is a creature of that society and gives her supreme
loyalty to God. However much she may believe in the way of

life of any given people—whether here or in Russia—she must finally serve God rather than men. It is her duty to carry the gospel to the ends of the earth. She is the Creature of the Great Commission which Christ gave his disciples long ago. Her power lies in the fellowship which men find with each other and with God in her common life as she seeks to do her divine duty.

You who are outside the Church are usually confused, if not repelled, by this barrage of claims. I will not pretend that it is an easy thing for you to get the "feel" of them by an objective survey of them. Yet you will be misunderstanding the Church constantly until and unless you make the effort and are at least partially successful in it. Once you do understand—whether you share it or not—the Church's conception of her nature and purpose, you will be in a position to appreciate many of the things she does. At least you will not say what an officer in the army told a group of ministers in Baltimore as World War II drew near: "It's all right for you men to protest against war now, but when it comes, you will just have to get on the band wagon!" He simply was unable to fathom a question that was immediately put to him, "Why? What difference would war make in the Church's duty to God?"

While you may not agree with the Church's conception of her mission if you do understand it, you are certain to misinterpret her if you do not understand it. Get a good grip on her sense of mission and you will know that and why she is different from schools, labor unions, fraternal and civic groups. She is the Church of God: that is her deepest conviction about herself—and, as you would understand her, you must understand that.

3. You owe her and yourself a clarification of why you are outside the Church. It is or ought to be regarded as an important matter to separate yourself from an essential part of

your heritage. Few of us would think of leaving home without having a good and sufficient reason. Not many of us would renounce our citizenship in this country without knowing why we were doing it. Only a few, a very few, ever seriously think of breaking away from civilization for life on an island in the South Pacific—and those who do are able to say why they do it. But half of the adults of America have cut themselves off from one of the most important parts of this heritage, and, I am afraid, the large majority of them are not able to give a good reason for their action.

Without in the least appearing to argue the case of the Church now, I want to point out the simple fact that you ought to be quite sure of your facts and quite clear about the adequacy of your conclusions before you either persist in your separation or separate yourself from the Church.

4. Finally, you owe the Church an honest effort to sharpen up and support your alternative to the Church. It may be a lodge, a club, a labor union, a political party to which you turn the energies which otherwise would find expression in the Church. But, whatever it is, you need to be clear in your own mind that it deserves and receives the same loyalty which the Church asks. You owe it to the Church to explain either why you think the work of the Church is unimportant or irrelevant, or why your alternative is better able to do this work than the Church.

Alternatives to the Church are not easy to find, I know. A classmate of mine in the philosophy department at the University of Chicago could not understand my interest in the Church, much less the ministry! He pointed to the Rockefeller Chapel one day and exclaimed, "They ought to stop all that foolishness that goes on in there and put the building to some good use." I was interested! And wanted to know what use he had in mind. He said, "Teach ethics, morals, philosophy—something worth while." Knowing that he was a relativist, I asked, "But what would you teach them in ethics that is really worth while?" He thought a minute, then said, "Yes, that is the problem. Until we get that figured out, we'd better let you fellows go ahead and use it."

When you choose an alternative to the Church, honesty requires that you admit that you would be willing to have the Church die. No consciously responsible man would be caught in the position of counting on the Church to continue her work, yet personally refusing to give her his loyal support. I wish I could rid myself of the feeling that the large majority of those who are outside the Church are actually caught in that position! If that is where you are, you owe it to yourself as well as to the Church to straighten out the matter one way or the other.

III

As I turn to the question of what you who are in the Church owe her, I think I shall simply remind you of the vow you took when you entered the Church—and let the matter rest there. You were asked, "Will you be loyal to the Methodist Church and uphold it by your prayers, your presence, your gifts and your service?" You answered, "I will." Study that for a moment and you may feel as did a young soldier who with his bride-to-be were listening to an explanation of the marriage vow: "I take thee to be my wedded wife, to have and to hold from this day forward, for better or worse, for richer or poorer, in sickness and in health, to love and to cherish, till death us do part." He swallowed hard, smiled wanly and said, "Say! That takes in a lot of territory!" I must say that a candid study of the vow we took on entering the Church does take in a lot of territory and much more than most of us actually give.

Your prayers: To be enough interested in the Church, to believe in her sufficiently, to love her devotedly enough to pray for her. If 600,000,000 churchmen the world around, if 3,500 members of the First Methodist Church of Evanston, Illinois, believed in prayer enough to pray, and believed with Tennyson that "more things are wrought by prayer than this world dreams of," and actually prayed for this Church, for the general Church, for all worshiping peoples of whatever faith—who doubts that there would be a revival of loyalty to the Church and a release of power in and through the Church that would prepare us for the task of being "the Church"? So far from being a lapse into the almost easygoing, all-too-ready preachment that "prayer can do anything," this is direct inference from the unarguable fact that the Church is a body of people brought together and bound together by loyalty to God. If that is so, then communion with God, both individually and collectively, is one of the fundamental rules of our common life.

Your presence: You owe the Church the interest, the effort and the time it takes to attend the meetings and services she sponsors. Every member of the Church ought to attend church unless prevented—and I mean actually stopped—by circumstances beyond his control. One of the greatest churches I ever knew was a small church in the Middle West with fifty-five members. When Sunday morning came they were in church. If fifty-two were there, the minister knew that three were sick or caring for the sick or out of town. We face no more important task in the life of a large church than that of building a high regard for and morale around faithful attendance at church services. I wish I could get the ear of every one of our thirty-five hundred members and say, "The Church owes you stated services of worship, and you owe the Church regular attendance at those services. It will be good for you and good for the Church to acknowledge and assume this mutual responsibility."

And I would like to sit down with the parents of the children in families of our church here in Evanston that are not now enrolled in our Church School and explain both our obligation to provide a good Church School and their obligation to make full use of it. The five hundred women who are members of the Church but not active in any phase of the women's work would have a right to object if we offered no such opportunity. Surely the Church has the responsibility of seeking to enlist their interest in a concrete way in this important part of our common life.

Some of you men have been hoping I would overlook you in this summation, haven't you? And I can not say I blame you very much because nearly one thousand of you are members of the Church and eligible for the Men's Club, but only a fraction of you attend its meetings. Do you realize what it would mean to this Church and community to have one thousand men actively at work in that Club? Can you think of a single thing that needed doing here that we would hesitate to attempt?

You who are members of the Church owe her your presence—your regular, conscientious, interested presence—both in the services of worship and in the part or parts of the program that are provided for you.

You promised her your gifts, too: And by gifts is meant ability as well as means. A Church like ours is all the richer for the commingling of town and gown in our fellowship. It is a good thing for specialists in theory and specialists in practice to worship, to think and to work together. Under such circumstances, the tendency for each to look down his nose at the other rapidly disappears. You owe the Church a share in the major interests and abilities of your life. Don't try to drop an iron curtain between the work by which you live and the reasons for which you live. Don't put work on one side and worship on the other and hope that "Ne'er the twain shall meet." It is the duty of the Church to see that they do meet, to bring them together in such fashion that they become a living whole and the ordinary work of ordinary people becomes sacramental in meaning—binding man to man and man to God.

Somewhere in her program the Church needs your talent—be it one, two or five, whether it is in some field of learning, some area of business, some special skill or some special achievement. We are the richer for all that the artists, saints and prophets have given us—and for the tens of millions of men and women who have laid their varied talents on the altar.

You owe the Church a share of your means. How much rests with you and your conscience. No one of us would either appreciate your trying to tell us or our trying to tell you what to give to the Church. This is both a free and a necessary form of stewardship. It is presented to you not as an assessment but as another opportunity for sharing in the life and work of the Church. The Church depends for the strength of her program upon the loyalty of her people. She is no mendicant, begging for her living, hat in hand. She has earned her right to seek your support. The Official Board of this and of every other Church need have no qualms about presenting the budget of the Church to you who are her members. And if they should have, they should recall the time William Rainey Harper, dynamic first president of the University of Chicago, was presented as "the greatest beggar in the world." He arose slowly and replied thoughtfully, "I never begged a dollar in my life—but I have given a lot of people great opportunities for usefulness."

Finally, you owe the Church your service: "Ah, there's the

rub!" for many of us. Most of the members of this church are busy people, and Evanston is the most highly organized community in America. Many of us are involved in so many good things outside the Church that we turn a deaf ear when the Church asks for our time. Not that she ever asks for all of it from many of us, but she does seek a share. Too few people set up the program of the Church for too many. Too few give generously of their time supporting and directing the program for too many. When I think of the hours on end I have seen some of you spend on the work of the Church *after your day's work is done,* and know that for every one of you doing that there are dozens giving little or no time to church work, I know I am in the presence of one of the persistent problems of a large church.

The initiative in this matter of the stewardship of time as well as money rests clearly with you. We hope you will offer your services freely to the life and work of the Church. And when the Church does seek a share of your time, we hope you will be able and willing to help.

One thing more—and probably the hardest of all—you owe the Church in the form of service. You must stand by her when the going gets rough! And it does get rough! The Church must proclaim the Gospel not alone as the way of life for the first century, but for the twentieth and every succeeding century. To do this, she must bring the life of her day before the judgment bar of the will of God as she finds it in Jesus Christ. She must be quick and fearless in her effort to awaken men to the error of their ways individually and collectively. This means that the Church must seek to interpret the gospel in terms of the gravest issues of our time. And, as she does this, criticism of her right to do it as well as the wisdom with which she does it is certain to come. This is where you come in. You ought to support her in this task; you ought to be one through whom she is able to do her work. When representative church bodies make a serious and humble effort to find the Christian way in and for our tangled world, they are going to level criticisms at social orders, at economic and national as well as international policies. I do not find it difficult to understand the protests which arise outside the Church when they do this, but I confess to bewilderment when it comes from within the Church herself.

You, as a churchman, owe the conferences of the Methodist Church, the National and World Councils of Churches, a decent and understanding hearing as they go about their—and your— duty. You need not agree with them and their pronouncements in order to be among those who defend their right to say what they say. The Church is supposed to lead, not follow, in the human search for the abundant life. A Church that seeks to be the lowest common denominator of public opinion is the lowest form of Church life. The Church does not for one moment believe that the voice of the people is the voice of God, nor that the majority is always right. She seeks to be law-abiding and to teach respect for civil authority, to be sure, but she has no hesitation in breaking with both law and authority when they seek to limit her freedom in proclaiming the gospel. Niemöller defied Hitler, Dibelius is defying the rulers of Eastern Germany—and both have done it in the name of the Church.

A part—an essential part—of your service to the Church today lies in your supporting her in her effort to be a power for good in our common life. Instead of trying to muzzle her, be one of the voices through which she speaks. Instead of going off mad when she says things you do not like, stick with her through thick and thin. If she is wrong—and she can be wrong—you will be *vindicated;* if she is right—and she has been right upon occasion—you may be saved.

IV

I have no fear for the future of the Church. She has outlasted civilization after civilization, and, should ours collapse, she will outlast it, and be the carrier of culture and the herald of the gospel to others to come.

> For not like kingdoms of the world
> Thy holy Church, O God!
> Tho' earthquake shocks are threatening her,
> And tempests are abroad;
>
> Unshaken as eternal hills,
> Immovable she stands,
> A mountain that shall fill the earth,
> A house not made with hands.

10 How Friendly Are You to the Church?

SCRIPTURE LESSON

Then cometh Jesus with them unto a place called Gethsemane, and saith unto the disciples, Sit ye here, while I go and pray yonder.

And he took with him Peter and the two sons of Zebedee, and began to be sorrowful and very heavy.

Then saith he unto them, My soul is exceeding sorrowful, even unto death: tarry ye here, and watch with me.

And he went a little farther, and fell on his face, and prayed, saying, O my Father, if it be possible, let this cup pass from me: nevertheless not as I will, but as thou wilt.

And he cometh unto the disciples, and findeth them asleep, and saith unto Peter, What, could ye not watch with me one hour?

Watch and pray, that ye enter not into temptation: the spirit indeed is willing, but the flesh is weak.

He went away again the second time, and prayed, saying, O my Father, if this cup may not pass away from me, except I drink it, thy will be done.

And he came and found them asleep again: for their eyes were heavy.

And he left them, and went away again, and prayed the third time, saying the same words.

Then cometh he to his disciples, and saith unto them, Sleep on now, and take your rest: behold, the hour is at hand, and the Son of man is betrayed into the hands of sinners.

Rise, let us be going: behold, he is at hand that doth betray me.

And while he yet spake, lo, Judas, one of the twelve, came, and with him a great multitude with swords and staves, from the chief priests and elders of the people.

Now he that betrayed him gave them a sign, saying, Whomsoever I shall kiss, that same is he: hold him fast.

And forthwith he came to Jesus, and said, Hail, master; and kissed him.

And Jesus said unto him, Friend, wherefore art thou come? Then came they, and laid hands on Jesus, and took him.

And, behold, one of them which were with Jesus stretched out his hand, and drew his sword, and struck a servant of the high priest's, and smote off his ear.

Then said Jesus unto him, Put up again thy sword into his place: for all they that take the sword shall perish with the sword.

Thinkest thou that I cannot now pray to my Father, and he shall presently give me more than twelve legions of angels?

But how then shall the scriptures be fulfilled, that thus it must be?

In that same hour said Jesus to the multitudes, Are ye come out as against a thief with swords and staves for to take me? I sat daily with you teaching in the temple, and ye laid no hold on me.

But all this was done, that the scriptures of the prophets might be fulfilled. Then all the disciples forsook him, and fled.

And they that had laid hold on Jesus led him away to Caiaphas the high priest, where the scribes and the elders were assembled.

But Peter followed him afar off unto the high priest's palace, and went in, and sat with the servants, to see the end.

ST. MATTHEW 26:36–58

I

A NUMBER of years ago the riders on the Fifth Avenue bus line in New York City saw the famous Old Brick Presbyterian Church being razed. The walls were finally lowered to the point where bus riders could look over them. One man won a good deal of notoriety for himself by observing, "That's the first time I've seen the inside of a church for years." Someone else, commenting on the incident, said that in all prob-

ability that fellow considered himself "statistically friendly to
the church." It is quite likely he would have been offended if
someone had inferred that he was not a Christian, or that he
was hostile to the Church, or that he was a liability to the
Christian religion. Yet all of these things might be true of him,
if we were to judge him by his comment.

I wish it were possible to by-pass as unimportant incidents
like these, but it would be utterly foolish to do so. We are living
in times when statistical friendship for the Church is not enough.
With mankind living through one of the most dangerous periods
in the long history, with the Christian churches the world over
locked in a mighty struggle with the evils which both persistently
threaten and periodically actually make this earth the scene of
immeasurable anguish and suffering, the Church is inclined to
say with her Lord, "He that is not with us is against us." We
number among our permanent problems injustice in every form,
malnutrition and famine, hatred and the entire war system. Once
more we behold the human family in the grip of civil strife of
every kind, and we cannot keep silent about it. Once more the
ancient dream of world peace and the brotherhood of man is
being shelved for a while in order that we may destroy one another. Confronting foes like these, you will understand the
Church's determination to know who is with her and who
against in the fateful struggle that now consumes her energies.

Make no mistake about this: the Church is not going to
surrender to these persistent enemies of God and man. She is
both engaged in the struggle now and girding up her energies
for an even greater struggle over the years ahead. Reaching
back to the very beginning of her great tradition as the Church
Militant, she is preparing to march forward under the unfurled
banner of her faith in God and in the Kingdom of God.
Obviously, one must believe in the message and mission of the
Church to want a place in her ranks in these days. There is

no place in that company for either the faint-hearted or the weak-kneed or the uncertain person. Statistical friendship will not do. Nor will friendship which exhausts itself in good intentions and well-wishing be of any great value. What the Church needs today is vital, sacrificial, creative, fearless friendship if she is to be strong for the struggle in which she is now heavily involved.

We have been living in a virtual war period since 1937—and it has been hard on everyone. These have been difficult yet glorious years for the Church. She has demonstrated a strength and sense of direction that have won the admiration of the world. Yet she cannot rest on her laurels. Sterner times lie ahead—as far ahead as the human mind can conceive. We are just now beginning to feel the full force of the shock and dislocation of one war coinciding with the shock and dislocation of a new war. Every social order in the world is threatened by disruption; every kind of government is either undergoing radical change or faces that possibility. Though the United Nations continues to be our best hope for world co-operation instead of world conflict, the great powers are turning away from the spirit and the use of it. They use it when it suits their private purposes, but their private purposes come first. With Asia finally aroused from Manchuria to Singapore, from Mongolia to India, and firmly determined to have a voice in her own destiny, with Europe frantically trying to rebuild her shattered life into some semblance of real strength, with Russia and the United States daily growing stronger in the most lethal weapons known to man and eying each other either for a false move or for an opening through which to launch a powerful blow—with this kind of a world on her hands, the Church must be pardoned if she asks you to inquire into the sincerity of your relationship with her.

That is what I should like to do now: conduct a kind of

clinic—with your co-operation of course—to enable you to determine just where you are in your relationship to the Church. Let me begin by suggesting a rough scale on which we can locate ourselves relative to the Church. Then, we shall consider certain questions which may help us understand why we are where we are on that scale. Finally, let me conclude the matter by stating what kind of strength it is the Church needs to do her job.

II

All of us belong in some one of three general groups relative to the Christian Church: nominal members; nonmembers but friendly to the Church; nonmembers but either unconcerned or actually hostile to the Church.

Consider, for a moment, those who are nominally members of the Church. As the name indicates, their names are on the records. They are on the mailing list, and the Church knows how to get in touch with them. She has some claim upon them and they upon the Church. She looks to them for support and they, for the most part, look to her for guidance and fellowship.

But not all nominal members are alike by any manner of reckoning. In fact, they fall into three well-defined groups. (1) There are the *vital members*—persons who give time, work and loyalty to the Church. They man her program: the various organizations and undertakings in her life. (2) Then there are the *casual members*—the once-in-a-whilers, so far as the church program is concerned. They attend worship services occasionally, or they work in some one of the various activities of the church sporadically. But—and this is crucial—they cannot be depended upon to help think, plan and work with any degree of steadiness in the total life of the Church. To put them on your official board is to load it down with so much deadwood. To ask them to serve as leaders anywhere is to commit the sin of asking someone who is only casually interested in the Church *as Church* to assume leadership in a vital phase of the Church's life. (3) Finally, among the nominal members of the Church are those who are plainly *inactive*. Their relationship to the Church is highly unsatisfactory from every point of view. It is maintained by occasional contributions, or by the presence of their children in the church school, or by the memory of their own childhood relationship to the Church. But they themselves no longer have the "feel" of the fellowship. They seldom if ever attend services of worship unless on Easter. Yet in response to a direct question, they would say that they belonged to the Church.

We come now to the second general group: those who are *nonmembers but friendly to the Church*. Here, again, we find that we must allow for certain differences among them. (1) We find those who, while not members, nonetheless attend church regularly. (2) Some attend church occasionally. (3) Then there are those—and their number is legion—who seldom if ever attend any sort of church service, but who, strangely enough, like to know that the Church is here and open, even though they, personally, want no responsible part of it. These friendly nonmembers constitute a considerable source of good will and support for the churches. Their good will is a strong outpost in the defenses of the Church in the community as she seeks to do her work. They can usually be counted on to rise to the support of the Church when criticisms begin to accumulate. Some of them give substantial contributions to the Church and take considerable pride in that fact.

The third general category includes those who are *nonmembers but either unconcerned about or actually hostile to the Church*. Once more certain distinctions will help us understand the true position of these people. (1) Prominent in the group are persons of another religious faith like Judaism or Islam or Buddhism. These, naturally, seldom come to know the Christian Church—though the Church is conducting missionary work among all non-Christian groups with real success. (2) Then we find those who never come, who know next to nothing about the Church, and who have no desire to learn more. (3) Finally, we encounter those who not only never come but who, in addition, are vigorously opposed for one reason or another to the Church and all she is trying to do.

As I indicated at the outset, this is a rough scale, but it may serve to help you locate yourself relative to the Church. When we take the most reliable statistical studies of the country and Church and pour them over this scale, we make some interesting discoveries about the people of our country and their Church relationships.

The bulk of people here fall into the first two groups: members and friendly nonmembers. Of our 150,000,000 citizens, some 75,000,000 are nominally related to some religious organization. From 4,000,000 to 5,000,000 are Jews, more or less in touch with the synagogues of their choice. Some 20,000,000 to 26,000,000 are in the Roman Catholic church. Approximately 40,000,000 have some identifiable connection with Protestant churches. Naturally we have no figures about the religious attitudes and habits of the remaining 50 per cent of our fellow countrymen, but it is safe to assume that a large majority of them are at least statistically friendly to the Church.

There seems to be a noticeable increase in several of the groups we were discussing a moment ago. And, I am convinced, these increases pose real problems for a Church facing the kind of challenge put to her by these days. For with these increases, the effective strength of the Church declines. Her nominal strength may continue, but her inner core of dependable members is weakened for their task.

We must note the sharp increase in the number of casual members—those who belong but whose interest is limited to and expressed by occasional visits to church services and occasional contributions to the church budget. It may be that we are more conscious of the numbers in this group because churches now keep their records of membership with greater care than formerly, but every church is painfully conscious of its size and importance. We must also be conscious of its meaning to the persons involved as well as to the Church. They simply are missing the vital, driving meaning of the faith that took the Gospel to the ends of the earth; they have somehow missed all connection with the real meanings of religion as the worship and joyful service of the living God. So far as the Church is concerned, their increasing numbers spell a serious loss of creative leadership and strength. Large churches as well as small ones find their work crippled not so much by outside criticism and opposition as by the lack of enthusiastic and consistent support on the part of many nominal members.

I should not be surprised to discover that there is a significant increase in the number of friendly nonmembers due principally to the heroic role which the Church played in Europe in World War II. Add to this the upsurge of Soviet Russia with her official doctrine of materialism and her record of opposition to religion, and it is easy to see why people opposed to her would exhibit a new and quite honest friendliness to religion. Even so, realistic churchmen will not be unduly comforted by this fact. It is one thing to welcome this new-found friendliness; it is quite another thing to try to build a program upon it. They bear about the same relationship to the actual processes of the Church as cheering spectators do to a runner trying to pick his way through a broken field. He may appreciate their presence and their cheers, but he knows that he must depend upon himself and his teammates if he is to get anywhere.

Still another group seems to be registering an increase in numbers over the last twenty-five years: the nonmembers who are openly hostile to the Church. Their given and announced reasons are well-known. On the one hand we hear radicals denounce the Church as hopelessly conservative. On the other, we hear conservatives say that they are pulling out of the Church because it is dangerously radical. Wherever the dogmas of communism get a hearing, religion is going to be denounced as an enemy of the people. And the ideology of communism has had a wide hearing the world around over the last few years. Wherever minority groups suffer oppression we are likely to hear the Church denounced (sometimes with real justice) as a tool of the majority. The missionary enterprise has been denounced in various sections of the world as a form of nationalistic imperialism, and the religious forces supporting the missions come under that condemnation, however unjust it may be. Manifestly, it is impossible to appraise the real strength of this increasing hostility to the Church, but we dare not pretend that it does not exist. Neither should be treat it as something new. The only effective answer to it is what we are.

There is one group that does not show anything like the sharp increase I wish were there and that is the *vital members*. By these we mean persons who are both affiliated with the Church and are influenced by a profound loyalty to its program, who regard it as having a just claim on their time, efforts and worldly goods. Not all are able to devote the same amount of these contributions to her program but they give conscientiously and to the limit of their ability. Let us put the present position of this group, numerically speaking, as carefully as possible. Church membership has kept pace with the growth of population in America, but the increase in vital members has not grown accordingly. We have larger churches without having a proportionately larger number of consecrated laymen to carry the planning and execution of the program.

If your initial impulse is to blame the Church for this situation, I would call your attention to the fact that the Church is largely a lay-enterprise and that you have laymen blaming themselves for the withering away of this loyalty to the Church. This, I believe, is uncomfortably close to the truth of the matter. We have been living through forty years of tremendous social, economic and international events. More weal and woe has been crowded into the life of this generation than used to be distributed over half a dozen generations. That may explain why the Church has been crowded out of the lives of some of the finest minds and rarest spirits of our time. They have given and continue to give themselves to causes that, at the moment, have an appeal to them that seems to outshine the glow of the ancient cause of the Church. Today, almost more than in any preceding day, the church program is severely crippled because so many members and friends have refused responsibility in the Church in order to devote their efforts to causes which might just as well be manned by persons who make no pretense of being members of the Church. I would like to confront those in our fellowship with what seems to me to be a tremendously important fact: there is no magic by which a Church can be kept vital and influential; that end is either won through the work or lost through the neglect of the laymen.

III

Let us turn now to the question of why you are where you are on this scale of relationship to the Church. It is possible to raise a number of inquiries that may help you understand that.

To begin with, how friendly are you to the *message* of the

Church? For the Church is not fundamentally a building or a social institution. She is a faith incarnate. At the center of her thought and life is a divine message and commission. Reduced to its simplest terms, this is the message: Jesus Christ is the clearest revelation of the will of God for the life of man that we have. In him is light and no darkness at all. He that hath seen him hath seen the Father. That is why the Church's primary question of men is, "What think ye of Christ?" That is basic. No vital fellowship in the Church is possible until this question is faced openly and answered in humble obedience to his will and way.

Is it not possible that we have here one of the reasons why so many vital members slip out into the category of casual members and keep right on slipping until they wind up as inactive members or nonmembers who are friendly to the Church? Insofar as they lose their belief in Jesus Christ as a vital fact for the minds, lives and relationships of men, it simply does not make sense to devote time and effort to church work. Insofar as they have a firm grip on his meaning for human life, they will throw themselves into the great work which he began and which he gave as the great commission to the Church.

Which raises the second question in this series: how friendly are you to the *mission* of the Church? Her mission is to present Jesus Christ as "the way, the truth, and the life." She confronts all men with this admonition: "Let this mind be in you that was in Jesus Christ." She cannot, she dare not, rest until she has made it plain to all men that only in him can they see their true relationship with one another and with God. Toward this end, then, she comforts the sorrowing, in his name; strengthens the weakening ones, in his name; stings awake our sluggish conscience, in his name. In his name, the Church believes in and works to be a fit instrument in the hand of God in the creation of His Kingdom on earth.

Obviously, a man must believe in the supreme importance of this mission before he can and will take and keep his place among the vital members of the Church. Let him, for whatever reason, begin to doubt that this message and mission of the Church is really essential to the common good of all men, and he will begin to slip away, notch by notch, on the scale of his relationship to the Church.

One more question I must ask: how friendly are you to the *fellowship* of the Church? By fellowship in the Church, I mean a group of persons bound together by a common loyalty to the will of God as we see it in Jesus Christ. That, I repeat, is the basic, the distinctive fact about the Christian Church. We who share in this fellowship lay no claim to perfection in either our message or the mission that grows from it. No one knows better than we do how unworthy of the task we are. I have frequently heard nonmembers express the strangest ideas about us. To hear some of them talk you would think we were a group of persons associating together for the express purpose of mutual self-deception on moral and spiritual matters.

What we try to do in our fellowship can be put quite simply: We are trying to measure our life and work against the standard for Christian living found in the life and teachings of Jesus Christ. None of us shows up very well in it, but we know it and are determined to be more faithful to it. We are driven, as it were, by an insistent conviction that this is the standard by which all men must measure themselves and their deeds if justice and peace are ever to come to mankind. By the various time-tested methods of worship, teaching and action, we seek to make our fellowship an informed, useful and efficient instrument in the hands of God as He builds His Kingdom on earth. In the services of worship we seek that kind of personal and social communion with Him that men have found to be indispensable to Christian living. In our smaller group activities, we seek to deepen the bonds of fellowship by deeds of service not alone within our own life but in our community and world.

When we are tempted to reason privately or publicly that we can be a good Christian without being a faithful churchman, a warning flag must be run up. Until a hundred years ago it never occurred to anyone to make the separation. And the evidence that we can do it today is still painfully lacking. From the very beginning of the Christian Church, the fellowship of Christians was "the body of Christ" on earth, to use a fine old phrase. To be separated from it is to be separated from Christ, and no Christian wants that. The nub of nearly two thousand years of experience in the matter can be put this way: significant Christians are vital churchmen.

IV

Humanly speaking, the Church depends for her strength and influence, not upon those who can be counted, but upon those who can be counted on. The strength of the Church cannot be gauged by the number of nominal members she has, nor by the number who frequent her services of worship upon occasion, nor by the number who think and speak well of her in our communities. Her life and strength are to be found in the solid core of consecrated vital members who believe in and are committed to her message and her mission. If there were any way to do it (and I confess I know of none antecedent to the trials of life itself), one could estimate her strength by the number of members who are determined to measure themselves and their day—even in critical times like these—by the mind and spirit of Jesus Christ. Such persons will not take their stand on the welfare of any one nation, or race or class. They will not ignore these, but they will subordinate them to the will of God as seen in the mind and spirit of Jesus Christ. They will not be afraid to echo Peter's sturdy words: "We must obey God rather than men." Such persons are the true pioneers of the Church, and they are needed as badly today as ever. When the Church, under God, can produce many such men the world over, she will be a mighty power for good in the councils of the nations and in the affairs of men generally.

One thing more—the most important of all—remains to be said about the source of the Church's confidence and strength. Her hope is in God. He has seen His Church through dark days before, and He can be depended upon to be a pillar of fire by night and of cloud by day as we seek to find His way for us through this confused and confusing world. Although we are surrounded by much darkness, He has placed an unquenchable Light on the further side of any valley of shadows through which we must find our way. And from that Light, even Jesus Christ, we get our sense of direction, our notions of right and wrong, good and evil, and toward that Light we make our way, confident that if we are faithful to Him, He will strengthen us for even greater trials than we are able to imagine.

This, then, is the crowning reward of vital fellowship in the Church—a sense of confident Oneness with Him who is the Father of all. From it will come the strength we need for the long hard pull in which we are now engaged, and from which we would not ask release even if it were possible to get it. For our purpose holds "to labor on," "to spend and be spent" in His name and for His sake. The Christian Church neither asks nor wants sympathy born of pity, but she does extend the hand of fellowship to you, and she will offer you a place where you can put your shoulder to the load.